CHATEAU TAHBILK

Story of a Vineyard
1860–1985

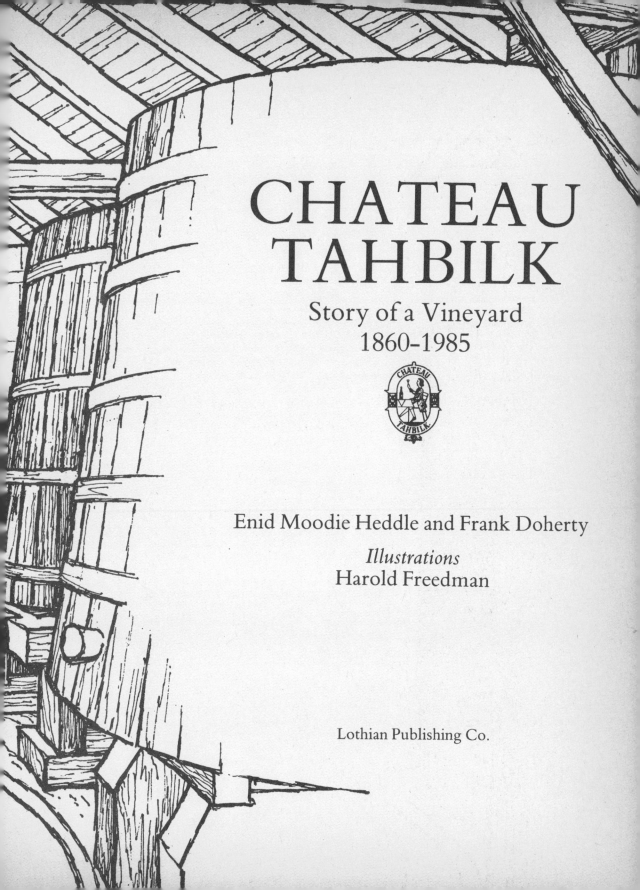

CHATEAU TAHBILK

Story of a Vineyard
1860–1985

Enid Moodie Heddle and Frank Doherty

Illustrations
Harold Freedman

Lothian Publishing Co.

Published 1985
by Lothian Publishing Company Pty Ltd

© E. M. Heddle, F. Doherty & H. Freedman
First published 1960 by F.W. Cheshire Pty Ltd

National Library of Australia
Cataloguing-in-Publication Data:

Moodie Heddle, Enid, 1904–   .
    Chateau Tahbilk, story of a vineyard 1860–1985.

    3rd ed.
    ISBN 0 85091 236 9.
    ISBN 0 85091 237 7 (pbk.).

    1. Wineries—Victoria—Tabilk—History. 2. Wine
and wine making—Victoria—Tabilk—History. I.
Doherty, Frank, 1916–   . II. Freedman, Harold. III.
Moodie Heddle, Enid, 1904–   . Story of a
vineyard, Chateau Tahbilk. IV. Title. V. Title: Story
of a vineyard, Chateau Tahbilk.

663'.2'0099454

This edition set by Alltype & Setting Services
Printed by The Dominion Press-Hedges & Bell
Cover design by Derrick I. Stone

The National Trust of Australia (Victoria) lists Chateau Tahbilk cellars among highly significant examples of early rural architecture worthy of preservation

The grape absorbs the sun
and the wine puts sunshine into men's hearts.

Foreword

Having followed the fortunes of Chateau Tahbilk for a great number of years I must pay tribute that it not only withstood the scourge of phylloxera—which devastated and subsequently wiped out so many other vineyards—but is one of the few vineyards in Victoria that has built solidly over the years upon its original foundation.

At a stage when its future was somewhat precarious, Tahbilk was fortunate enough to obtain a new owner—perhaps not well versed in viticultural lore—but abundantly endowed with courage and initiative. Fighting a hard up-hill battle, and devoting much energy to the task, Mr Eric Purbrick succeeded in bringing about such a metamorphosis of vineyard and cellar that prospective buyers were forced to acknowledge that here was a source of supply not to be lightly regarded.

Congratulations to Eric Purbrick that today he is the owner of one of the largest and most important vineyards entirely devoted to the production of light table wines. Knowing him, it is certain that Tahbilk will not be content to rest on its laurels, but will take for its slogan 'Quality, and yet more quality'.

T. C. Seabrook
1960

My dear friend, the late Tom Seabrook, was gracious enough to write an introduction to our original book and to comment on the good fortune of Chateau Tahbilk when I came to the Estate in 1931. Be that as it may, no-one realizes more than myself the tremendous good fortune that Chateau Tahbilk now has in having two more generations carrying on the Purbrick tradition—my son John and two grandsons, Alister and Mark; maybe there will be a great grandson to carry Tahbilk's tradition a generation further.

At this stage, most of the responsibility falls on the shoulders of Alister, who is the Managing Director of the Company, as well as its proven winemaker.

Eric S. Purbrick
1985

Contents

Introduction

Australia, an old country with a short history, is full of tales of human effort which in the last hundred years has so changed her landscape. Here I have tried to tell in outline, from original sources preserved at the homestead and elsewhere, the fascinating story of Chateau Tahbilk; to show how this Victorian vineyard came to be set down in one exact spot on the banks of the Goulburn River in 1860, how it grew, and why it looks as it does today with its mile-long avenue of olives, and white mulberries, approached by an old wooden bridge across the backwaters of the Goulburn where platypus still live and wild duck and black swan sail sedately up and down. North of Seymour the road winds towards this bridge which leads the visitor to the chateau-like tower, rising above the trees of orchard and cellar-yard, familiar to thousands of Australians only as seen on wine bottles with the Chateau Tahbilk label. Here is the story behind the label: of what is over the bridge.

I have been able to trace this story only with the co-operation of the present owner of Chateau Tahbilk and of members of families connected with it in the past. I should like here to express my particular gratitude to:

The Trustees of the Mitchell Library for permission to use extracts from the Horne papers and from the first number of The Sydney Gazette; Mr J. Purbrick; Mr H. Parris; descendants of Thomas Hutchins Bear (Mr and Mrs R. W. Bear, Mrs G. A. M. Bear and her daughter, Mrs B. McLean); Miss Isabella M. de Soyres; C. de Pury, Esq. of Yerinberg for permission to quote portion of a letter from Charles Joseph Latrobe and for his making accessible to me family correspondence which Mrs Robert Koner kindly translated into English for me; the de Castella family for extracts from letters of Francis de Castella; Dr Brian Elliott who located certain of the R. H. Horne papers; Professor S. J. Butlin for information on The Melbourne Banking Company; R. G. Casey, Esq., for permission to reproduce an inscription from a wine-goblet; and lastly, Mr and Mrs Eric Purbrick of Chateau Tahbilk, at whose invitation the story was written, who generously made available the Tahbilk vineyard letter-book and other records held at Chateau Tahbilk.

ENID MOODIE HEDDLE
Part One

There was never anything arduous about my writing an account of Chateau Tahbilk's progress so far into its second century; it fitted happily and easily into that category headed by that over-worked (but accurate) old cliche—A Labour of Love.

To me, love is not too strong, too flamboyant a word to use about anything pertaining to Chateau Tahbilk, for it, its incumbents and its surrounds have held a special place in my affections for the best part of all these twenty-five years. I have loved the way of the place—the timeless, gracious homestead, the unique cellars, the long—unrequired but historic—stables, the beauty of the winery yard in Autumn with its russet and golden carpet, the quiet tranquillity of the whole bushland haven—with a steadfastness that has never weakened.

It has been a privilege, too, through that quarter-century to count the Purbrick family as special friends who have been a constant source of assistance and inspiration.

As for its wines, I can only aver with complete truth that I am a 'strong Tahbilk man' from way back.

One can do no more than hope that whoever writes the next contribution to Chateau Tahbilk's history will find it as easy and rewarding a task as I have done.

FRANK DOHERTY
Part Two

PART ONE

THE FIRST
HUNDRED YEARS

The Story Begins with the River

Long before white men found the valley the river was at work
cutting and shaping the land with strong probing waters, shearing
through red clay, sifting fine sand and coarse sand and, in flood
years, reaching out far beyond the confines of the high, curving
banks which kept its flow within bounds in normal seasons to spread

wide layers of rich brown mud over the valley slopes. Through the centuries swampy lagoons and curving billabongs along the valley filled and dried and were filled again. Here the wild duck bred and many other water birds. Platypus made homes along the river banks and clusters of black swans sailed up and down on the broad waters, undisturbed except when small parties of aborigines ferried themselves across stream in their bark canoes on the way from one camp to another. The whole length of the valley was good hunting ground. There were big fish in the river and bronze-winged pigeon among the tall gums bordering the main stream. Kangaroos and emus ran in the forest; there was plenty of wood for campfires and water always, even in the dry seasons. There were good canoe-trees growing in the bush near the river, and hidden corroboree grounds lay among the islands standing in the billabongs.

Bayunga the aborigines called the river and they had names for the water-holes and billabongs—Deegay, Tatura, Nagambie, Bontharambo.

Sometimes the tribal hunters set the bush burning or summer lightning lit great fires in the dry seasons which blackened the gum trees and eat up the tangled undergrowth. Winter storms felled many tall trees on the burnt-out slopes and good grass grew there when the rains came.

To the Major's men, when they set eyes on these park-like spaces in the tangled bushland, the valley looked fine country for flocks and herds. On this day, 7 October 1836, they had done fourteen miles. Now they were setting up camp for the night. Through the long valley, entered the day before, meandered a deeply cut stream-bed containing a chain of ponds. Near one of these the Major ordered Barrett, his overseer, to begin the unloading of the gear from the drays. As he stood watching a pair of cockatoos with scarlet and yellow top-knots flew screeching across the camp from the direction of the ponds. Piper, the Sydney blackfellow, came up soon afterwards with news that a party of aborigines was following in their tracks. Barrett went out with Piper to persuade them to

2

come up to the camp. Seven aborigines soon appeared and the Major himself hastened to meet them for he did not want them to 'sit down' too near. Three of them carried neatly wrought baskets for which he gave them two tomahawks. He then returned to his tent, making signs that it was time to sleep but, before they moved off to rejoin their tribe, the 'old man' among them told Piper the creek watering the long valley was the Deegay. Nearby was the great Bayunga.

Since leaving Sydney in March, with a party of twenty-five men, his gear on drays and his two boats on their boat carriage, Major Mitchell, Surveyor-General to the Colony, had been more than two thousand miles, exploring mountains and streams and investigating the geological character of the land through which he passed. By this survey, he wrote in his journal, he hoped 'to develop those natural advantages certain to become of vast importance to a new people'.

When the Major's party camped overnight at the Deegay Ponds, their long overland expedition on its way to completion, the small settlement on Hobson's Bay, where John Pascoe Fawkner's party had arrived on 11 October 1835, was yet two days off its first anniversary, the city of Melbourne still scarcely more than a pioneer's dream.

On 9 October Mitchell's men crossed the Bayunga, which white men were to call the Goulburn, after meeting with a broad, dry channel or lagoon with lofty gum-trees of the 'yarra' species on its borders. A fine river they found it, somewhat larger than the Murrumbidgee. Mitchell recorded in his journal that, as it was nowhere fordable at that time, he 'sought an eligible place for swimming the cattle and horses across and immediately launched the boat. All the animals reached the opposite bank in safety; and by the evening every part of our equipment except the boat-carrier was also across. . . . At exactly $2\frac{1}{2}$ miles from the river the outer bank was reached and the straight course homewards resumed through level forest country grassy and good, open enough to give the men a prospect of about a mile around'.

The Major's journal recorded his thoughts on the land near the Goulburn being suitable for pastures and his visualisation of his and his men's footsteps 'soon being followed by men and animals'.

Those of his expedition going direct from Portland Bay in charge of Mr Staplyton actually met at Gundagai the first overlanders making for Port Phillip, droving stock from the Sydney side. By the time the Major's men reached Sydney on 3 November 1836, having covered 2,500 miles in seven months, the overlanders were well south on the track which soon came to be known as the Major's Line. While Major Mitchell was camping at the Deegay in October these first overlanders gathered by appointment at Howe's station on the Murrumbidgee where Mr Joseph Hawdon had mustered and brought in cattle for droving south. At that time land was taken up as squatting stations along both sides of the Murrumbidgee. Now, in the beginning of the dry weather, the overlanders began to follow the Major's tracks back to the Goulburn and, where the wheels of his drays had cut deep tracks in the wet season, theirs 'moderately loaded did not make a mark'.

John Hepburn, who accompanied Joseph Hawdon on his trip south found the huts of Batman's settlement at Port Phillip 'only slabs stuck in the ground forming a roof and covered with earth'. He counted 'several horses and but fifteen head of cattle there'. On his return to Sydney, however, he found Port Phillip was attracting so much attention that 'to keep up the excitement' he wrote a letter to the editor of the *Colonist* newspaper suggesting the possibility of running a post between Sydney and the new settlement in the south. In fact, he put forward plans for the first overland mail run from Sydney to Melbourne.

I laid down all the stages from the Murrumbidgee to the settlement, with estimated distances, and showing how easy it was to provide hay—grass was then so abundant at any point. The Governor Sir R. Bourke took up the matter. No questions were asked; tenders were issued and taken up by Joseph Hawdon, after

4

much delay, so that the first overland mail, carried on horseback from Melbourne by John Conway Bourke, for Hawdon, left on 2 January 1838.

In the meantime, Hepburn had decided to go to Port Phillip himself to settle. On 15 January 1838, he left New South Wales 'with 1,400 ewes, 50 rams, 200 wethers, 2 drays, 18 bullocks, and 10 men, all prisoners of the Crown'. He took also '1 cart and horse, 1 saddle horse, 2 brood mares, private property and Mrs Hepburn and two children'. Following the tracks of those who had gone before them was not difficult and soon they came onto the Major's Line. Following it they reached the Goulburn and, passing through fine-looking country, crossed the river on 2 March 1838 'all safe without any molestation from the natives'. Here they overtook Mr John Harrison and Mr Hamilton who had pushed on to get the choice of the country. 'We assisted these gentlemen to cross their sheep. Hamilton advanced and we took a day's rest on this beautiful spot; to be known to the early settlers as Old Crossing Place.'

'No other shepherds crossed the Goulburn up to this date,' Hepburn later wrote to Governor Charles Joseph Latrobe, 'but the station-holders A. Mollison, C. H. Ebden, Captain Brown, Harrison, Coghill, Bowman and myself.'

Soon after this, John Clarke applied for a licence to establish a Public House on the Goulburn River. The licence for this, possibly the first outside Melbourne, was granted in a letter dated 4 June 1838 from the Colonial Secretary's Office in Sydney to the Police Magistrate at Melbourne. On 11 June this letter was followed by another stating that the Government was 'desirous of seeing Houses of Entertainment established on the road between Port Phillip and Yass; and that facilities will be afforded for this purpose by selling small lots of land (not more than five acres) in convenient situation', but no land was to be sold within four hundred yards of the bank of a river lest it interfere with the future establishment of a ferry or the building of a bridge.

5

Clarke's Inn was set about half way between Old Crossing Place, where Major Mitchell had sent his equipment across the Goulburn, and the crossing later to be used by the Sydney-Melbourne mail coach; directly opposite what was soon to be known as the Tabilk run.

By the end of June the Governor had considered a letter from the Deputy Surveyor-General suggesting that, in addition to such Houses of Entertainment, 'townships should be established with as little delay as possible at the several points where the Road (between Yass and Port Phillip) crosses the following streams—viz. 1. The Murray 2. The Ovens 3. Violet Creek 4. The Goulburn'. The Police Magistrate's orders were 'to take measures for carrying this into effect in order that Post Houses, Police Stations and Houses of Public Entertainment, as well as Ferries if necessary be established at these several points'.

The Colonel commanding Her Majesty's troops was also requested to 'co-operate in the Establishment of Military Posts on the roads'. Sixteen mounted police and eighteen infantry, it was suggested, would be required of which three troopers and eight infantry would be needed for the Goulburn area. Major Mitchell's country quickly began to take on a new pattern.

By 1837 Government plans for Aboriginal Protectorates were being made. The Goulburn Protectorate was set up a little below Old Crossing Place, quite near the Major's camping spot, by James W. Dredge, a schoolmaster from Salisbury in England who arrived in Melbourne in the barque *Hope*, out of Sydney, on 3 January 1839. On 21 May he wrote in his diary, 'A shepherd has been murdered by the blacks on the Goulburn so hope to be off tomorrow'. His gear was loaded on a bullock dray and his men, two ex-convicts on parole, wore corduroy jackets, trousers, shirts, hats and shoes, which he supplied for £1.5.0 per man. On 22 May he wrote, 'Left Melbourne 2 p.m. on Billy [his horse which had cost £50 in Port Phillip]. 26 May Pitched tent on bend of river a little above Clarkes''.

Here he built a hut, getting the blacks to cut bark for his roof as it

6

leaked so badly. By Christmas he had peas, beans, cabbages, carrots and potatoes from his own garden, although it had been a hard summer in 1839 after a long drought of seven months. Though he quickly succeeded with his garden, James Dredge had so many other difficulties that he resigned and the protectorate was moved further down the river nearer to Murchison.

In the September of 1839 Charles Joseph Latrobe had arrived to take charge of affairs in Port Phillip. Now, in 1840, the Manton Brothers came north to take up land on the Goulburn in the area known as Carrick O'Shannassy, with a head station named Tabilk. Their first homestead here may have been the troopers' barracks— the quarters of the first six police to be stationed on the Goulburn, just opposite Clarke's Inn at Old Crossing Place. The line of red gums which were probably planted near these barracks by the first police troopers stationed on the Goulburn, and which still stand on Chateau Tahbilk land to this day, were very young trees when the Mantons came. In a letter written in 1853 Governor Latrobe was told that the Mantons 'occupied both sides of the river including almost the whole from there to the Murray'. They had the station known as Noorilim from 1840 to 1842, and Old Crossing Place from 1840 to 1846.

When this run was divided into two by the Mantons the Tabilk, or No. 1 run, was taken up by John Purcell and Henry Moore who applied to the Government for 8,500 acres at Old Crossing Place (Tabilk) in January 1848, claiming they had been in residence there for at least three years. On 8 August of that year Henry Moore wrote Latrobe stating they had in fact occupied the run since 1842.

By 1850 there were 71,000 people in the Port Phillip district and more than a million sheep. Country for nearly two hundred miles round Melbourne was under cultivation or used for pasture by station holders, especially along the line of road to Sydney. After the Colony of Victoria was proclaimed in 1851, 29,076 acres of Carrick O'Shannassy was among Crown Lands thrown open for selection, 'on or after September 1852.' This year Hugh Glass, an

7

Irishman of wide interests and abilities, who had been in the Colony since 1840, joined John Purcell in leasing the Tabilk run.

Hugh Glass began his career in Port Phillip as a stock and station agent. He moved about the country and acquired properties in so many parts of the Colony that he was soon one of the largest land-owners and the richest men in Australia. He built himself a mansion at Flemington with its own private zoo in which he collected birds and animals native to Australia, he imported thoroughbred fillies from abroad, he became a member of the Legislative Assembly.

Soon after joining Purcell Hugh Glass applied for permission to purchase the Pre-Emptive Rights of 640 acres, or one square mile of the Tabilk lands, and this was granted on 13 October 1856.

Sheep and cattle continued to be run on his land as had been done ever since the first overlanders camped there on their way south from the Murrumbidgee but, as the result of the mysterious disappearance of Andrew Sinclair, a neighbouring squatter living on the Noorilim run, a vineyard was to be planted on the river valley slopes of the Tabilk run in 1860.

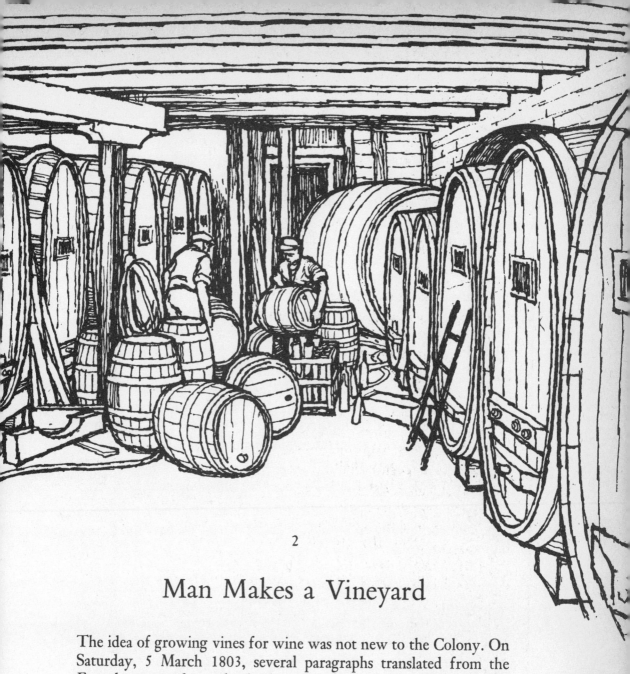

Man Makes a Vineyard

The idea of growing vines for wine was not new to the Colony. On Saturday, 5 March 1803, several paragraphs translated from the French appeared on the back page of the first number of *The Sydney Gazette* on the method of preparing a piece of land for the purpose of forming a vineyard:

The Ground is to be turned up, cleared of weeds, and trenched out, to the depth of 18 inches; or, should it not be encumbered with stumps or roots of trees, underwood, or brambles, the cuttings of vines may be immediately planted without that precaution . . .

For the purpose of planting the young vines already rooted, holes are to be made with a strong hoe, or broad pick-axe, at a discretionary distance of about 2 and a half or 3 feet open from each vine, and some mould or old turf must be lain round the foot of each.

The method of dressing the vines after the vineyard being formed, is principally to prune them well, and to attend to a minute knowledge of their nature; also what influence the change of climate may have operated on them: some will not produce without being propped, others best without; and the situation of the land and temperature of the climate will determine if the branches are to be carried more or less in height, and consequently how to be supported; they may be cut off either in a flat or sloped manner, but care must be taken to clear away all dead or defective parts.

By 1830 James Milson was writing from the North Shore to complain to H. Donnison, Esq., of Bligh Street, Sydney, that Donnison's pigs were continually trespassing in his orchard 'and have done considerable damage among my valuable Grape Vines'—but in the Port Phillip district, where settlement came so much later than round Sydney, there were but 3½ acres under vines by 1842. These may have included the vines at 'Jolimont' planted by Charles Joseph Latrobe, himself, in the garden of what was to be Victoria's first Government House, as well as the vines grown at 'Mayfield', the home of the McCrae family where Georgiana McCrae entered in her journal on 9 August of that year—

Mr Latrobe came to show Osmond how to plant the vine-cuttings 'obliquely to the sun, each cutting to have three joints and "eyes"—one of these to be above ground, the second level with the surface, the third to be rubbed off to make way for the root'.

Mr Latrobe had learnt to handle vines in Switzerland at Neuchatel where he had lived when in his early twenties. Neuchatel was the home of his wife—Sophie, daughter of Frederick August de Montmillon, Swiss Councillor of State, and Rose de Meuron. During his years in Neuchatel the young Latrobe visited Jolimont, the country estate of the de Montmillons, set on a wooded height about two thousand feet above the lake of Neuchatel. There he fell in love with Sophie and, as well, came to know many members of the families of de Meuron, de Pury and de Soyres and some of the young vignerons connected with the Swiss wine industry. People from Neuchatel, closely connected by ties of kinship and of friendship, were soon to develop the wine industry in Victoria.

Latrobe advised Clement Deschamps, son of the head vigneron of a Swiss vineyard, to migrate to Port Phillip and Amiet's wines, listed among beverages served at a fancy-dress ball given on 28 November 1850, to celebrate the separation of Port Phillip from New South Wales, were made in the Colony by another Swiss—husband of Rose Pelet, daughter of Latrobe's housekeeper.

Latrobe was a man of varied interests. Before the publication in 1829 of *The Alpenstock*, his sketches of Switzerland, he went mountain climbing there, being the first Englishman to reach certain passes in the Swiss Alps. Later he travelled across the Atlantic to the United States on the same ship as the American writer Washington Irving, who described him in his *Tour of the Prairies*—'Mr L. an Englishman'—as 'a man of a thousand occupations; a botanist, a geologist, a hunter of beetles and butterflies, a musical amateur, a sketcher of no mean pretensions; in short a complete virtuoso . . . never had a man more irons in the fire; and consequently never was a man more busy or cheerful'.

When Latrobe was busying himself with the affairs of the young settlement at Port Phillip vines were not only being grown at

13

'Jolimont' and at 'Mayfield'. Skene Craig, Commissariat Officer of the Port Phillip Department, had a vineyard in Collins Street West. More important than these plots of vines, however, were those grown at Dalry, for here were settlers from Neuchatel whose business was wine-growing. Here, almost certainly, early plans for a vineyard on the Goulburn were discussed; later, from Yering were to come technical advice and trained managers for Tabilk.

When, in 1860, some of the most influential men in Port Phillip, including 'the Right Worshipful Mayor of Melbourne', met to draw up plans for establishing a company to plant a vineyard on the Goulburn, the gold rush which had brought many newcomers to the Colony had slowed down. By 1854 the bush country through which Mitchell's expedition had passed was dotted with diggings, active or abandoned.

By the lonely lagoon of Warranga a gold commission camp had sprung up and there were others at the Fenced-in Water-holes, at Whroo and at the Old and New Main Gullies' Camp, rechristened Rushworth by Commissioner Horne. Here the aborigines of the Bayunga carrying long wooden spears, waddies and bark shields, watched silently the hordes of searchers for gold hidden in the river sands and the 'commissioners, inspectors, captains, sub-inspectors, lieutenants, cadets in silver lace and embroidery, capering about on splendid horses' from one new diggings to another, setting up gold-office tents furnished with mahogany tables, great brass scales and weights and iron safes to be filled with the white men's treasure and guarded by pacing sentries, in military red, 'with musket and fixed bayonet'.

Among those who came to the diggings at Whroo was Ludovic Marie, a Frenchman born in Burgundy. Marie arrived from Bordeaux with a collection of goods from Europe to start a business in Melbourne. He journeyed to the goldfields at Ballarat, Castlemaine, McIvor and Whroo and decided to settle on the Goulburn. When the first hotel licences were issued for the goldfields Marie opened a hotel and store, at Whroo, and applied for a licence to operate a

14

punt at a convenient spot for travellers crossing the river in a straight line from the Ovens. His licence, issued from the Colonial Secretary's office in Melbourne on 30 August 1855, gave him permission to operate the Murchison punt and to charge 'the following rates of fares (and no greater):

For every Foot Passenger	1/-
For every Horseman	2/-
For every Horse-Team	4/-
For every Bullock-Team	7/-
Cattle per head	2d.
Sheep under 100	5/-
Sheep exceeding 100	2d. each'

In 1859 Marie went off to the Indigo Rush at Chiltern where he was said to have been the first to use steam machinery. By then he was a well-known figure on the Goulburn. Not only did he run the Murchison punt and his business at Whroo but he held the post of manager on the Tabilk run for Hugh Glass. In the garden of the homestead at Tabilk he proved that vines would grow swiftly and produce massed bunches of table-grapes. He seems to have experimented also with cuttings of wine-grapes, for the existence of these at Tabilk was to be mentioned in early advertisements announcing plans for a vineyard on the run.

One of the business acquaintances Marie made on the goldfields was Richard Henry Horne, an Englishman who had left a literary career in London to make his fortune in Australia, though advised against this by Charles Dickens for whose magazine *Household Words* he was then writing.

Soon after Horne landed in Port Phillip in 1852 he secured the post of commander of the gold-escort from Ballarat to Melbourne. In the following year he was appointed gold-commissioner on the Goulburn. Horne wrote later that after about twelve months at this work over 'a wide sprawling district of empty graves, recently golden gullies, quartz hills, lush, savage forests, mournful lagoons and miserable swamps' where he was more than once awakened at daybreak by a distant rippling sound to see his slippers float from beneath his bed, some of the creeks having risen in the night and flooded the whole camp, he obtained leave of absence for five weeks and set out for Melbourne.

Stopping for a night's rest, and to get my horse shod, at McIvor, I found there was to be a land-sale next day. I looked at the plan—saw the 'new township of Murchison' on the banks of the Goulburn River—noticed the 'site of the bridge', and made up my mind to bid for river-frontages opposite that bridge, and to have them. I knew the locality well: it was adjoining the station of the 'Black Protectorate' (meaning a place where blankets, tobacco, bread and other articles were periodically given to the aboriginal tribes of that locality); and as I had continually swum across the river at different points, I knew the land well on both banks. But some of the diggers knew the land better than I. . . . In addition to this there was a little vengeance, and a good deal of fun, in bidding against a commissioner. So they 'ran me up' for every choice allotment to the absurd extent of 70/- per acre for land on a wilderness, one hundred and twenty-five miles and upwards from Melbourne. This was in 1854.

Horne had been known in England as author of *Orion*, a poem of 3,000 lines in blank verse on the advancement of man, but he had many interests. Scarcely an odder figure can be imagined among the many eccentric gentlemen who came to the Melbourne of gold-period days. A pile of pocket diaries he used in Victoria between 1854 and 1865 lie now in the Mitchell Library in Sydney, along with other personal papers of his. The diaries record business dealings with Ludovic Marie and others in Victoria, as well as social engagements and his literary work for Dickens's magazines and *The Cornhill*. He notes payments received for a lecture tour in 1861, when he spoke to audiences in Brighton, Geelong and Ballarat on how to succeed in life; his asking 'several people including Charles Dickens to procure me the Professorship of English Literature at the Melbourne University through Sir R. Barry in London'; his lonely bush rides on his horse, Victor; and his sending of copies of 'my advertisement for 1,000,000 vine cuttings' to Thackeray.

From his papers, and from old Melbourne play-bills, we discover Horne was a keen amateur actor, playing John Dory in a Melbourne performance of *Wild Oats*, as well as writing a special prologue for the play. He wrote, too, a Cantata addressed to 'H.R.H. Prince Alfred, Duke of Edinburgh on his first arrival in the Colony of Victoria'. Interested in music he never travelled without his guitar. When he felt like playing on this he did so, not only at polite evening concerts but in the middle of Bourke Street on a Saturday morning.

His activities were not confined to the arts. He had studied electricity with some attention and, of its future, he wrote 'enthusiasts have projected machines for travelling in the air—the time shall come when men shall not merely use the air as a great highway for travel to any part of the globe but shall pass through the sea in fish-like ships at the same pace as the larger fish, regardless of the weight of the cargo'.

He was one of the first men in the Colony to suggest the building of a railway to Seymour and the clearing of snags in the Goulburn to open up river traffic to the Murray. He suggested utilising the flesh of the kangaroo for home consumption and export 'instead of destroying it wholesale and leaving to rot the indigenous food of the people'. He recommended the cultivation of the mulberry for silk-worms and the cactus for the cochineal-insect. A well-known figure in the capital city of Victoria, he was to be met in the town houses of Melbourne bankers, merchants and politicians as well as at station homesteads along the Yarra and Plenty.

He stood for Parliament and, although not elected, in October 1858 he was appointed to a Select Committee set up by the Government of Victoria to inquire into the properties of the Yan Yean in

17

connection with the improvement of Melbourne's water supply. On 24 January 1860 he was appointed to another similar committee. This month he was also actively interesting himself in the formation of the Goulburn Vineyard Proprietary, 'a company for the cultivation of the vine and the making of wines on the banks of the Goulburn River'. On 7 January *The Age*, Melbourne, contained an advertisement setting out plans for the company and giving as its provisional committee J. G. Dougharty, R. H. Horne, N. R. D. Bond and A. Sinclair, Murchison. Deposits of 10s. per share were to be sent to the Company's brokers, Wray and Bryant, 63 Temple Court; or to A. Sinclair, Murchison, from whom the company proposed to purchase the Noorilim run.

Ludovic Marie wrote from Murchison to Horne on 16 January 1860, signing himself 'Manager of the G.V.C.':

'I shall commence to lay out the ground tomorrow in blocks of 20 acres and let each of them by contract to clear for the plough.' In a postscript on the back of this letter Marie added 'on the success of your movements will depend the fate of the company. It is intended to close the share list by the 15th of February and have the first call by the 10th of March so you will have no time to spare. We trust in you, Yours very truly, L. Marie.'

The proposed capital of this company was to be £30,000 in shares of £5 each, limited liability. A deposit of 10s. per share was to be paid on application; £1 on allotment; £1 in June 1860; £1 in April 1861; £1 in April 1862; and 10s. in April 1863, but the whole plan depended on Andrew Sinclair's sale of Noorilim Station to the Company. As the prospectus stated, 'Here a substantial property, the pre-emptive rights of the Noorilim Station containing 640 acres, on the Banks of the Goulburn River has been offered to the Company at a price very moderate, considering the value of the land in the neighbourhood, the numerous advantages of the station (which has a river frontage of two miles, in addition to the fact that 400 acres

18

are already in a fit state to be planted with vines), and also that the proprietor has taken 1,000 shares in part payment—or about five-sixths of the whole amount'.

Anticipating this sale, the minutes of the meeting held on 16 March 1860 'at the offices of John Hood Esq. (house)' and recorded in Horne's handwriting, showed that it was resolved to form a company to be called the Goulburn Vineyard Proprietary, 'Resolved that Mr Ludovic Marie to be the manager of the works resident on the Goulburn, that Mr R. H. Horne to act as honorary secretary, pro tem'.

Purchase of the Noorilim estate was considered and determined and the salary of the manager of the works was fixed at £750 per annum. To show his confidence in the undertaking Mr Marie proposed to receive his salary in the following manner—£400 in cash and £350 value in shares during the first three years. The Board accepted the proposal, 200 shares to be reserved for the purpose. The services of the manager of the works being at once required, it was resolved that an advance of £5 per week be made to him, to be submitted at the first general meeting of the shareholders.

The prospectus drawn up for the company, and prepared for printing by R. H. Horne, remarked 'that Victoria is a country eminently adapted by nature for the cultivation of Vines, is a fact that has long been generally known. The means we possess here of making wines of the most delicious quality, and better suited to the inhabitants of these colonies as a healthy beverage than most of the light wines which are imported has also been equally well-known to those who are conversant with the subject. The wines of the Rhine and the Moselle can certainly be equalled, but in some instances will probably be surpassed, by vintages of the Goulburn, the Loddon, the Campaspe, and, in fact, of the whole valley of the Murray. . . . Besides the commercial benefits, the best sanitary and moral results may be anticipated, because a wine-drinking population is never a drunken population . . .'.

'Dr Ferdinand Mueller, the Government Botanist,' it added, 'has expressed his sympathy with the undertaking and kindly promised any advice that may be required.'

An advertisement printed at the *Standard* Office, Chiltern, on 17 January stated 'the quality of grapes produced by the few stocks at the garden and at the house is an indubitable proof of the capabilities of the ground. The expenses of the first year will be £14,915, which includes the purchase of the whole estate together with the planting of three hundred acres with vines'.

However, the Melbourne *Argus* of 29 May 1860 reported the inquest on the body of Mr Andrew Sinclair at Brighton after it was found in the scrub opposite Mr Webb's residence, Brighton Park. The story of Sinclair's last days was told some years later by Horne in this way—

Mr Sinclair came down to Melbourne to arrange terms with the proposed Company. He was a bush-gentleman who liked the usual sort of brandy, caring nothing for wine but wishing to make the most of his land. On the first day of his arrival, being at dinner at Bignel's hotel, some colonial wine was recommended to him as being very fine. It was one of the pale golden Kaludahs. He drank the first glass, and looked thoughtful; then a second glass, and looked round, as though he fancied we were all laughing at him. Somebody asked what he thought of it, for it was really a beautiful and delicate wine. 'Well,' he said, 'I think that a glass of sherry in a bucket of water, would represent all its qualities,—so far as my taste is concerned'. A day or two afterwards Mr Sinclair was missing. Nobody knew what had become of him. 'Off on the spree!' it was said. At the end of two or three weeks the unfortunate gentleman's body, disfigured by insects, reptiles, and the native cat, and dissolving in the sun, was discovered in the scrub of the sea-shore near St Kilda, where it appeared that he had wandered after having been hocussed by some brandy he had drunk at one of the evil villas of the suburbs.

Unfortunate as Andrew Sinclair's disappearance and death were,

Horne was not to be diverted from his plans although an advertisement drafted by him had already appeared. 'In consequence of the sudden disappearance and probable death of the proprietor of the Noorilim Station,' it read, 'the intended purchase of the land for the proposed company has lapsed. The Provisional Directors and shareholders of the proposed company of the Goulburn Vineyard Proprietary are requested to meet at the Argus Hotel, Collins Street, at 12 o'clock sharp on Saturday the 4th instant, with a view to the formal dissolution of the proposed company afore mentioned. R. H. Horne, Hon. Sec. G. V. P.'

It was obvious that the location of the vineyard must be altered. Horne immediately set to work to arrange to transfer its situation to the adjoining Tabilk run, in which Hugh Glass was interested. One very important result of this change was the inclusion among directors of the new company of John Pinney Bear and his brother Thomas Hutchins Bear.

The Bears had arrived in the Port Phillip district in October 1841 on the ship *Brothers* chartered in London by their father, and his friend Captain Dunsford, to bring to Australia their families, servants and labourers, their sheep and pigs, 'a Durham cow in calf' and certain goods likely to be saleable in the Colony.

The Bears had held land at Tiverton in the estate of the Earl of Devon.

A journal kept by John Pinney Bear from June 1840 to October 1841 describes the last months he spent in Devon and the record of the voyage to Port Phillip. John Pinney kept a Field Book and was an able surveyor and map-maker, though still in his teens. 'Did a map for the Earl of Devon,' he noted. 'Measuring lines all day and finishing measuring the land on the East side of the main line in the Week Manor portion of the Land. . . .'

His family's interests are shown as extending beyond farming to clothes of some elegance, to literature and to the theatre. 'Father paid Retallick tonight for making a velveteen coat for me,' he

21

John Pinney Bear

recorded; and 'Father bought Mother a velvet cape with a hood to it'.

When John Pinney went to London with his father to make final preparations for sailing to Australia he visited Westminster Abbey and 'saw there the tombs of several kings of England and other distinguished characters . . . saw also the Coronation chairs, the one in which Queen Victoria was crowned. I sat in it.' He visited the National Gallery and 'saw all the pictures', then on to the Pyrotechnic Exhibition. He also went with his father 'to some friends of Mr Duncan's wine merchants went in their Vaults and had some wine'.

A capable lively youth, not yet eighteen when his family arrived at 'Williams Town' on Wednesday 20 October 1841—'thick, hazy

22

day, rather cold strong breeze'—John Pinney remained on the ship to supervise the landing of his father's cattle 'and put them aboard a boat when it came alongside'.

The last hastily written entries in his journal give impressions gained after sighting Cape Otway. 'October 18. . . . We are all much pleased with the harbour and coast around and hope the interior of the country will equally gratify. . . .' The pilot expects cyder 'will sell well also Champagne and Brandy meet with a good sale; potatoes £18 per ton, labour is very dear a man gets from 5/- to 6/- per day, and sawyers 14/-. Very fine warm day.'

On 20 October he concentrated on the interest he found in the new telegraph at Williams Town. 'The news of the arrival of ships is quickly conveyed from this to Melbourne by means of a telegraph, they hoist their number coming in and it is telegraphed to Melbourne in 5 minutes.'

A man of some wealth, John Bear was knowledgeable about farming and experienced in dealing with stock. The stock and station agency he set up in Melbourne prospered and his sons soon held the stations Yan Yean on the Plenty and Serpentine on the Loddon.

Soon after settling in Port Phillip, John Bear experimented with wine growing. William Westgarth mentions in his *Australia Felix* receiving from him 'a few bottles of his Port Phillip champagne manufactured from the pure juice of the grape'; and Frederick Race Godfrey's journal for 1849 describes a drive to the Plenty, in December, when 'John Bear was there and we had great fun broaching his Australian wine which was so good it made us all merry'.

After his father's death in 1851 John Pinney carried on the family business in the city, himself laying with a silver trowel, on 1 January 1866, the corner-stone of a new building for the Melbourne Banking Company, to house his business headquarters in Queen Street. Thomas Hutchins ran Yan Yean Station on the Plenty River and was half-owner with his brother of the Serpentine on the Loddon. Later he was to be one of the directors of the National Bank of Victoria, as well as director of the Tabilk Vineyard Company.

Hugh Glass had business connections with the Bears and R. H. Horne had met them before he approached Glass with his plans for a vineyard on the Tabilk run. In 1854 and in 1856 the Victorian Government had twice purchased portions of the Yan Yean run in connection with the water supply scheme for Melbourne. Horne's idea for establishing a vineyard may have followed visits to Yering, near Bear's run, where Paul de Castella had settled in 1850 and planted a vineyard in 1856. In 1859, the year in which Horne was busy with plans for a vineyard on the Goulburn, de Castella imported plant and 10,000 vine cuttings for Yering. Both Horne and the Bears would have heard of the purchase for they had friends in common in Melbourne. It is tempting to suggest that de Castella's success at Yering was spoken about at the Melbourne Club in the presence of Horne or the Bears and that the establishment of the vineyard on the Plenty encouraged the Melbourne magnates Horne wanted to interest in a similar venture on the Goulburn. But we do not know who actually arranged for the meeting most important for our story, which Horne's pencil notes record was held on 6 June 1860 at 70 Queen Street 'for the purpose of forming the Company to be entitled the Tabilk Vineyard Proprietary'. We do know that in connection with this meeting, which did actually establish the vineyards, Horne had an advertisement inserted in *The Age*, Melbourne, which read:

> To Vignerons—Gentlemen who are fully qualified by practical experience as vignerons and willing to undertake the management of a vineyard company on the banks of the Goulburn are invited to send their names by one p m 8 inst to Tabilk Proprietary, 70 Queen Street, R. H. Horne, Hon. Sec. T.V.P.

At the meeting a letter from Mr L. Marie was read, 'making certain claims for services performed', and it was suggested 'that the sum of £25 be offered to L. Marie in view of all demands—carried'.
This proposal was submitted and accepted for Marie had already laid out in detail the programme for establishing a vineyard on the

Noorilim run. His rough notes are preserved among Horne's papers. They give a time-table for one year's work, showing he had practical experience of wine-growing. He would need, he considered, '25 men to be constantly in the works' during the fifth year of work.

> May June July—pruning and tying the prongs from 10.15 extra men, required for 2 months July August hoeing
> September—cellar work, drawing of the wine made in March
> October—disbudding employ extra hands October and November tying shoots—then another hoeing
> December and January disbudding again and cutting the tops of the shoots
> January—One week to spare for crops of hay
> February getting the press ready cleaning casks and vats etc.
> March gathering.

On Tuesday 3 July the Provisional Board for Tabilk Vineyards Proprietary met again when Mr Robert Morrice from the Whipstick Diggings presented himself as candidate in the office of manager of the works. He stated that he required '£300 per annum with rations and residence'. The meeting put questions to him on vine culture which had been put to other candidates and then 'adjourned to Thursday night the 5th instant at 3 o'clock p.m. for the purpose of finally deciding between Mr R. Morrice and Mr L. Marie for the appointment of manager of the work'. The secretary was authorised by the Board to offer Mr R. Morrice £1 per day for two days' further detention in addition to £10 for his expenses in coming from the Whipstick Diggings.

On 5 July an offer was made by the Board to Marie of £200 per annum 'with house accommodation and rations, subject to an increase of £25 per annum—the salary to be paid monthly and the arrangement to be terminated by a month's notice on either side to commence from this day. Mr Marie accepted the appointment but asked the board to record on its minutes a recommendation that the question of a bonus to him (Mr Marie) should be considered at the expiration of four years from this day (if he remained in the service of the company)—this was agreed to be recorded'.

The manager was directed 'to propose forthwith' a list of the vine cuttings he would require, and to state what operations were necessary for immediately commencing the work. 'This was done and the Board adjourned to tomorrow, Friday the 6 July at 2 o'clock,' when Marie received more instructions from the Committee.

1. The manager to keep a Diary
2. To furnish a fortnightly report of proceedings to the Directors in Melbourne
3. All accounts to be paid by orders drawn on the secretary in Melbourne of which advices were to be sent.

Then Mr J. P. Bear, always a man with large ideas, proposed that 'an advertisement for one million of vine cuttings be inserted in *The Argus*, South Australian *Register*, *Sydney Morning Herald* and Geelong *Advertiser* six times in each paper'.

The Secretary was directed 'to telegraph to Sydney and Adelaide in pursuance of the foregoing resolution, every day being now of importance'. Later, Horne wrote that he 'advertised for 1 million of vine cuttings from all the Australian Colonies, which were obtained, the best of them planted by a highly competent vigneron, and 700,000 took root and produced grapes the first year'. It seems doubtful this report was entirely accurate for Horne constantly exaggerated, but the advertisement was for a million cuttings.

When the newly formed company with a capital of £25,000 took over on 1 August 1860 the 640 acres of the Tabilk run purchased from Hugh Glass for £5.10 per acre, the land was covered with gigantic gums and scattered patches of honeysuckle. There was an eight-roomed dwelling and stables on the run but, as well as clearing and preparing the ground for ploughing before planting vines, labour had to be provided for excavating and building a cellar on the river bank, of stone quarried on the estate. Everything else needed to provide for the first vintage had to be made on the spot or purchased and brought from Melbourne or from Sydney by bullock wagon or coach.

By the end of 1860 150 acres had been cleared under Marie's direction and 65 acres planted. Horne, who was at Tabilk during 1860, helped to plant vine-cuttings when the ground was ready. He worked in his usual bush costume of wide-brimmed 'wild-west' hat, a loose scarf tucked in the neck of his shirt, which he wore with the tails outside his pants. In these clothes he could hope to wield an axe in comfort, as would not have been possible in the long-tailed coat, enveloping waist-coat, high collar, carefully tied cravat and tall stovepipe hat he wore in Melbourne. As he watched the felling of the yellow box along the valley slopes he may have been aware that the land on which such trees grow was suitable for planting the deep-rooted vine, for, like the box, the vine requires a deep, penetrable subsoil.

Marie was still in his late twenties and Horne already fifty-seven but he put all his spare time into helping the young vigneron through the first months of clearing and planting. However, the main responsibility for maintaining the vineyard was to be taken by John Pinney Bear and his brother-in-law, A. R. Noyes, who succeeded Horne when he ceased to be 'secretary pro tem'. In time the ownership of the vineyard was to pass into the hands of John Pinney Bear whose family business it finally became.

A visitor who described the vineyard in 1861 in the Kilmore *Examiner* estimated that 200 acres were under vines 'all of them healthy and free from blight'. Some two dozen men were at work and new ground was being cleared. 'A small quantity of wine is expected to be made this year, next year actual operation will commence. The dwelling house has been completely renovated and some additions in the shape of offices erected on the bank of the river.'

But difficulties did have to be faced. Marie left in 1862 and this year seems to have been a bad one for wine-growing in Victoria for

27

Charles Joseph Latrobe, living in retirement in England, wrote then to Guillaume de Pury of Yeringberg, who was visiting his family at Neuchatel—

I should be glad to know how you have got on, and what your prospects and those of your brother may be. I hope and I trust with reason that you at least, have been disconnected for some time with de Castella and Anderson's firm. I have no pleasure in reporting other people's misfortunes and particularly not those of anyone in whom I have always felt so much interest as in de Castella—and you will have probably heard from other sources by the February mail just arrived, of the astounding failure of that firm for an amount which would appear to place hope of arraynt and recovery quite out of the question. What a pity! ...

Latrobe might equally well have been foretelling the failure of Hugh Glass, one of the major shareholders in the original Tabilk company who was to die in 1870 nearly penniless, although this was due to his other ventures rather than to Tabilk affairs.

Between 1861 and 1875 the company set-up of Tabilk Vineyards was reorganised several times. In 1862 Sands and McDougalls' *Melbourne Directory* listed under general companies—Tabilk Vineyard Proprietary—office 68 Queen Street, Secretary A. R. Noyes; and the same up to 1866. In 1877 the company was listed as Australian Freehold Land and Produce Co. Ltd, Drewe, W. S. Secretary, office 85 Little Collins Street East. The Australian Vineyards Pty Ltd was formed to acquire the assets of the Tabilk Vineyard Company 'including presses, vats, stills, tubs, casks, tools and chattels, together with the stock of wines and spirits of the vintage of 1865'. Subscribers, all with ten shares each, were J. P. Bear, banker; H. Glass, merchant; T. H. Bear, squatter; J. E. Blake, gentleman; A. Ryan, stock-agent. F. Reed and J. Filson, estate agent and accountant, were the first auditors. John Pinney Bear was chairman, his brother-in-law Arthur R. Noyes, secretary to the company. Marie having left in 1862 to start another vineyard, J. E. Blake, who had experience of wine-growing in New South Wales, leased the vineyard for a time. In 1870 a young Swiss gentleman was appointed resident manager.

Leopold Quintin de Soyres was of 'Madame' Latrobe's family. A grandson of that Baron Leopold de Meuron who had reached England during the French Revolution and there married a lady of George III's court, at sixteen de Soyres shipped as a midshipman in the 870-ton *Seringpatam* to Bombay and back. He made a voyage to the East Indies before his first voyage to Melbourne on the *Roxburgh Castle*. There he returned to settle, after several years as officer in the merchant service on the West Indian run. His aunt, Julie, from Neuchatel had given him an introduction to Mr Paul de Castella, at the Melbourne Club. Like the de Pury brothers,

R. H. Horne at Tabilk

29

Guillaume and Samuel, who had come earlier from Neuchatel to Port Phillip, young de Soyres began to look for a place to plant a vineyard. He worked at Yering with de Castella and de Pury and then took the post at Tabilk after a plan for a partnership in a vineyard with de Pury, suggested by his friend George Langdon in London, failed to materialise because he was unable to raise the money he needed to pay for this.

By the articles of agreement made on the twenty-eighth day of April 1870, the company agreed 'to hire and engage the said Leopold Quintin de Soyres of Melbourne in the Colony of Victoria, Gentleman, as Manager of the Tabilk Vineyards, cellars and lands situated on the Goulburn River in the said Colony from the first day of May one thousand, eight hundred and seventy, at a salary at the rate of two hundred pounds per annum, payable monthly, plus ordinary board and rations for himself and a married couple'. He was 'to reside upon the said vineyard' and 'not to waste the property of the company nor suffer any damage to be done thereto'. The agreement was terminable at a month's notice from either party.

What was Tabilk vineyard like when young de Soyres arrived as manager? By the end of 1860, according to a visitor from Avenel who wrote a description for the Kilmore *Examiner* in January 1861, the vineyard itself had been enclosed by 'a substantial three-rail fence', the homestead was undergoing extensive repairs and rebuilding, the orchard 'immediately attached to the house' was in excellent order. 'Here the vines of some years' growth are literally groaning with grapes. I also observed some very beautiful apples, peaches and pear trees. . . . Separated by a fence is the nursery, which looks remarkably green, it is traversed by surface drains about 30 yards apart, these joining channels to take off the surface water . . . and new ground is being daily cleared. . . . All the vines look healthy and free from blight; upwards of two dozen men are at work. . . . A small quantity of wine is expected to be made this year, next year actual operations will commence.' The men employed were mostly French and Italians.

30

By May 1870 more clearing and more planting had been completed and wine-making was in full swing. Offices had been erected on the river bank, where the ornamental trees and shrubs planted since 1860 were rapidly growing up. A 'horsepower machine' for pumping water from the Goulburn for irrigating purposes had been set up on the river bank (at the combined suggestion of Ludovic Marie who loved steam-engines and R. H. Horne who was strongly in favour of irrigation from the river); but the Avenel visitor was told it had remained unused because of the awkwardness of its situation making it liable to be flooded whenever the river rose after heavy rain. It had been removed before de Soyres came.

A huge cellar had been excavated parallel to the river, and on its bank. This was one of the largest in the Colony, some 300 feet in length and built of stone quarried on the estate. All the great beams used in its construction were cut from timber grown at Tabilk. The cellar stood about 35 feet above the summer level of the river and it was the Company's hope that, when the Goulburn began to be navigated after snagging—which R. H. Horne had advocated on every possible occasion—casks of wine intended for conveyance to Melbourne by way of Seymour, or to Riverina where there was a considerable sale for colonial wine, could be 'dropped from the cellar onto a steamer or barge with the greatest convenience. The vineyard might expect to enjoy the double advantage of river and railway communication in the future'.

Near the cellar, with its pressing rooms above, small stone cottages for the labourers on farm and vineyard began to be built, each with its fruit and vegetable garden. These with the carpenter's shop, the stables, and the blacksmith's shop, the store, the butchery—where the mutton and pig-meat, grown on the farm attached to the vineyard, was hung for manager's and labourers' rations—gave the group of riverside buildings the look of a pleasantly lively little village, Leopold Quintin de Soyres thought as he walked between the two rows of young planes bordering its 'main street' on his first tour of inspection as manager. He felt that he would be able, here, to put all

31

his plans for being a successful vigneron into practice very happily.

By 1871, however, he had begun to be worried about his prospects at Tabilk, although assured by Arthur Noyes, secretary to the Company, that there was no alteration in his engagement thought of as a result of changes in management. 'You will please look after the whole wine and property for the interest of all concerned,' Noyes added; but de Soyres left in 1872 to go into partnership with a Mr Playford in the Major Plains Store at Dookie. Receiving a legacy from his mother he was finally able to plant his own vineyard at Dookie and to buy a run at Glenrowan, as well. Three months before his sudden death, at the age of 43, he visited Tabilk and was able to inspect the new cellars, which had been completed in 1876, the pagoda-like addition to the end of the old cellar, the French 'grappoir' used at vintage by his successor, Francois de Coueslant, who had much more to show him in the way of improvements to Tabilk than he expected to find there. Now that the new manager had given the old cellar its chateau-like addition the little settlement reminded him more than ever of a village in the vineyard country of Europe.

In 1879 the Victorian *Gazette* had noted among its list of Victorian vineyards 'The Tabilk (or as it is now called *Chateau Tahbilk* vineyard)'. The new title was charmingly suitable. We have, unfortunately, no record as to who was responsible for it. Was it due to a suggestion from de Coueslant or to an instruction from John Pinney Bear influenced by his travels in Europe? Tantalisingly, we never discover this, although the vineyard records for 1879 are detailed in every other respect.

Francois de Coueslant had been resident manager since March 1877 and was regarded by all the wine growers of the Goulburn valley, and as far away as the Murray vineyards and the Government Experimental Farm at Cashel, as a most knowledgeable vigneron and a progressive farm-manager. Before de Coueslant left his own vineyard at Wormangal to take on the responsibility of Tabilk, William Ford, a Melbourne chemist who went into partnership with John

32

Pinney Bear to buy the estate after Hugh Glass died, had lived at Tabilk for several years, being followed by a Dr Adams who was newly appointed resident manager when Mr Bear laid the corner-stone of the new cellar on 1 January 1876.

Ford and Bear had begun showing their wines and the products of the vineyard following the 1873 vintage which the *Nagambie Times* had reported as being 'no less than 25,000 gallons'. The new cellar, for which W. A. Zeal of Melbourne was architect and the contractor James Purbrick of Seymour, not, however, related to the Pur-brick family which was later to own Tabilk vineyard, began to be excavated towards the end of 1875. Purbrick tendered for the

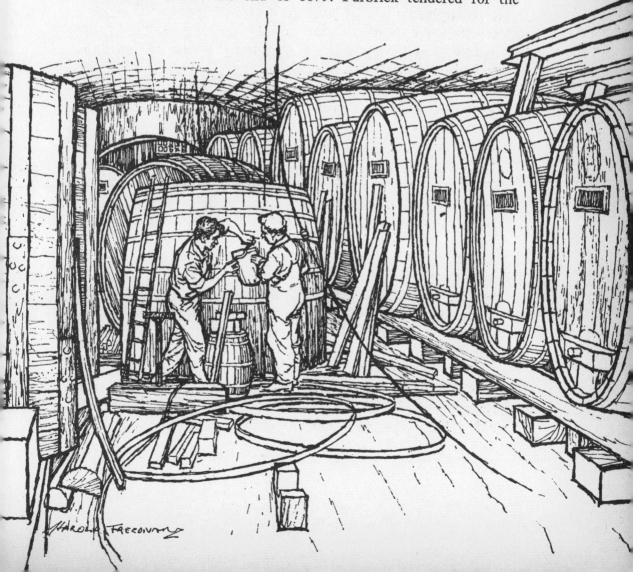

excavating contract following the appearance of an advertisement in *The Goulburn Valley Advocate*, circulated in the districts of Mangalore, Tabilk, Avenel, Seymour, Wahring, Murchison, Toolamba and Shepparton.

TABILK VINEYARD

PICK AND SHOVEL WORK

TENDERS received till 26. inst. for REMOVING about 2000 cubic yards of EXCAVATION FOR CELLAR

Particulars at vineyard

The lowest, or any tender, not necessarily accepted

11 October 1875

The architect's specifications for excavation, hand-written on a blue folio sheet, ruled feint and water-stained, with rough calculations jotted down on its reverse side, still exist.

The excavation was to be 'in the form of the sketch underneath'.

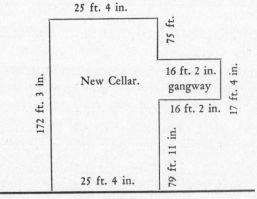

Very precise instructions were given for the removal of the earth and its layering 'in three foot levels or benches trimmed on its outer edge to a uniform slope of about 2 to 1 from a level line on the timber framework which protects the old cellar from the floods of the river Goulburn'. The contractor was to provide 'all and every description of tools labour and materials, also horses, drays barrows planks etc. which may be required' and 'shall carry on the work with despatch so as not to retard the progress of the brick layer'.

In spite of many complaints by the architect and the vineyard management about Purbrick's methods and rate of work, Bennet, then resident clerk, was able to report to the Company's Melbourne office on 2 December 1875—'Purbrick is making good progress with the new cellar. He is down about nine feet'; and on 16 December, 'the first brick will be laid tomorrow, I believe'. These bricks had actually been burnt on Tabilk land and, although the closing date for tenders had been advertised as 26 October 1875, the big job of excavation was apparently completed before the new year.

When laying the corner-stone Mr Bear stressed that the new cellar would be completed in time to receive the 1876 vintage and Tabilk would then possess cellarage capacity for nearly two hundred thousand gallons of wine. The last two vintages, he said, had produced nearly 140,000 gallons and this year looked as promising. The company's estate had been extended by the purchase of adjacent farms which were being subdivided into smaller paddocks and laid down with artificial grasses. The ten acres at Sherry Bend where C. H. Ebden, one of the first overlanders, had camped in 1838, was now one of the most productive parts of the vineyard, having produced 11,000 gallons of wine last season, so surprisingly large a quantity that we suspect Mr Bear was exaggerating.

The Nagambie *Chronicle* which reported these remarks went on to say 'a vase containing the daily and local journals, and a scroll recording the event, together with two bottles of Tabilk wine, were then placed in a cavity in the wall, and the stone having been lowered into its place, and the square, level, and mallet properly applied, the stone was declared by Mr Bear to be well and truly laid'. After which followed the toast 'success and prosperity to Tabilk and abundant vintages and full cellars'; and 'all the men present were regaled with a plentiful supply of good red and white Tabilk'.

Soon after the 1876 vintage was gathered Mr Ford died in Melbourn and the direction of affairs at Tabilk fell entirely on John Pinney Bear.

Francois de Coueslant came to Tabilk in time to take charge of the 1877 vintage. An authority on the vine, his *Treatment of Vines* points out that Tabilk vineyard was let out in blocks to Swiss and German vignerons when he took over. These cultivated blocks according to their own systems, under contract, without any regard to local conditions. This was common in Australia at that time. 'Wines are made in Europe in obedience to local conditions,' Hubert de Castella wrote in *John Bull's Vineyard* in 1886. 'Australian vignerons are imported from all countries and have methods each of his own province.' Tabilk vineyards, under de Coueslant, were to be dealt with very differently. Francois de Coueslant was to try many experiments but he, himself, was to do the detailed planning and direct the execution of all work done. He was as interested as ever R. H. Horne and Ludovic Marie had been in new machinery, whether for use in farm or vineyard.

'I am always ready to try new experiments because it is the only way to make progress. So I am always willing to help others to do the same,' he wrote to Joseph Knight of Kialba who sent for cuttings from Tabilk in 1882. He held long discussions by letter with the managers of the State Experimental Farm at Cashel on methods of planting, cultivation and irrigation. From the State Farm he also obtained olive cuttings to plant out with the idea of establishing an olive oil industry. Earlier he had planted white mulberries—a long double avenue leading to the homestead settlement—with some hope of establishing a silk industry in Victoria. He planned to employ the wives and daughters of his vineyard workers to handle the silk-worms and to spin the silk from the cocoons when ready but this

36

plan, like that for growing olives, failed to materialise. Only the clumps of dark leaved olives scattered about Chateau Tahbilk and the long, double avenue of light-leaved mulberries leading to the present homestead settlement remain to remind visitors of these de Coueslant innovations.

And he was most disgusted when Mr Bear wrote from London that French vignerons would not use the crusher and egrappoir. 'I dare say they might not, in the estate of things, but if they had to pay the same wages that the Australian vignerons have, they would have to change their crawling system or their pocket would have to suffer from their foolishness. The perfection of implements does not mean deterioration of wine; although some French vignerons might think it.'

De Coueslant was always interested in 'the perfection of implements' as much of his writing shows. A letter-book preserved at Chateau Tahbilk holds copies of correspondence sent out between 1875 and 1883 from the vineyard. It contains copies of de Coueslant's letters from the date of his arrival there and so we know what he did and thought from day to day, as well as when the new cellar was dug and its great arched roof of brick completed, what business was discussed with Mr Bear when he was away in London, what rations and equipment were needed from Melbourne, how the work of farm and vineyard went on from one season to another, what rains came and when the river rose and fell, what stocks of wine and wool accumulated, who the vineyard's customers were, which wines de Coueslant recommended as suitable for gentlemen and which for ladies, what was bought and whether this went to the customers by rail, by barge on the Goulburn or by Cobb and Co.'s coach making its routine trips round the valley.

We know what tools Peter Sullivan, the cooper, used, how casks and fences were made and cottages built on the estate, when fire came from Pearce's paddock, that Chinese labour was best for contract clearing, that the blacksmith at Avenel was able to make a fine

37

'three-furrows vineyard plough' but that 'the wheels from Johns' in Melbourne were no good.

'That fellow must be an ass from head to foot! Among the wheels he has sent up there is 4 tramway wheels perfectly useless to me.... When I sent down the other wheels I sent a *pattern* with them, but I suppose he did not think it worth his while to look at it, because the 4 he sent up have nothing in common with it, except the centre hole, if it was in the middle, which it is not.'

We hear what trouble men cooks were, especially at vintage, what married couples were good or bad workers, what advice was given to neighbouring settlers who were anxious to establish their own vineyards, the fate of the farm horses and sheep and pigs, as well as the progress of the vines, experiments and routines of wine-making, preparation of wines for exhibition in Paris and for sale in London.

The letter-book tells the daily history of Chateau Tahbilk as de Coueslant brought vineyard and farm to the peak of achievement reached there in the nineteenth century. We also see clearly what country life was like in the Goulburn valley in the eighteen-eighties.

Wines being made at Tabilk when de Coueslant arrived included riesling, verdielho, pedro, muscat, hermitage and malbec, cabernet, burgundy, gonaris, ancorat, shiraz. There were also some spirits and liqueurs. Wine names listed in the company letter-book include pascorata, a name coined to describe a sweet white liqueur wine quantities of which were sold between 1878 and 1883; but most of the wines' names are of classic wine-grapes imported from Europe into the Colony when wine-growing began in Australia.

On 12 March 1877, the day before vintage began, the resident clerk, Mr Browne, and his cellarmen signed a statement of stock of wines, spirits and liqueurs which distinguished the quantity of the different vintages held in gallons, the total being 92,158 gallons. There were 256 gallons of spirits and 278 of liqueurs.

The 1876 vintage of 35,000 gallons, with an additional 557 of liqueurs, cost £265.6.6 which included wages of cellarmen and coopers, carters and pickers (both men and boys), butcher, chief cook and three assistant cooks; along with rations (about £100) and horse feed.

In preparation for this vintage the clerk at Tabilk sent a memo of wanted articles to the Melbourne office.

3 dozen common forks (table) for hut
3 dozen pannikins (for Hut)
1 large fork to take meat out of boiler
1 skimmer for boiler
3 dozen com. Pocket knives for cutting grapes
1 dozen tin buckets for cellar
65 feet of manilla rope for cellar
3 scrubbing brushes for cellar

1 gall of sweet oil for cellar
150 feet large hose with 6 couplings
3 lb. of copper wire (sample of which I shall send)
Red carrot seed (for garden)
Parsnip seed   „   „
Turnip seed   „   „
Tomato seed (large)   „
2 bags Ration Sugar about 27/-
1 box Tobacco @ 3/- or 2/6

A drum of boiled linseed oil is required 'for Peter Sullivan to oil his casks'. Also required are a few cases of salmon and lobster, tea, cocoa, rice, oatmeal, sago, gunpowder and shots, epsom salts, sugar —white and brown (we learn that 'ration sugar' was brown). 'If you can send some of other kind of white sugar than the crystallised one. Nobody likes it here. The last brown sugar was very good,' the clerk notes on his order as an afterthought.

In all the 1878 vintage cost £250.18.0—£100.11.8 for rations and £150.6.4 for wages.

A printed note preserved in the Chateau's records about this time sets out regulations and rate of wages per day during vintage at Chateau Tahbilk.

CELLARMAN	3	0	per day
DRUMMERS	2	2	„
CARTERS	2	0	„
MAN PICKERS	1	8	„
BOY PICKERS From 1 0 to	1	8	„
HEAD COOK	3	6	„
SECOND COOK	2	6	„

Anybody leaving before the Vintage is finished will be paid at the rate of SIXPENCE UNDER the above rate of wages.

* * *

SHALL BE DISCHARGED AND ALSO PAID AT THE RATE OF SIXPENCE UNDER THE ABOVE RATE OF WAGES:

1. Anybody detected neglecting his duty.
2. „ „ pelting at others in the Vineyard or Cellar.
3. „ „ remaining in the Kitchen after Meals, unless in rainy weather.
4. „ „ creating Disturbance about the Premises after 9 p.m.
5. „ „ sleeping in the Yard of Stack Yard.
6. „ „ smoking in the Dormitory, or making any modification to the Bunks therein.
7. „ „ drawing caricatures or writing names on the walls, doors, or tables.
8. Anybody wishing to be Discharged must give 24 hours notice to his overseer, or lose 24 hours wages.
9. No Wine will be Sold or part payment made during the course of Vintage.
10. The store will be open during 15 minutes from 7 p.m. on WEDNESDAY and SATURDAY.

'I have been very much hindered in the gathering by the rain,' de Coueslant wrote, 'and I have lost an amount of grapes. There would have been more than 30,000 gallons if it had not rained.'

On 12 May 1878 he wrote to Mr Bear—

'As it was understood before you went away I had the rails for the new fence cut at the other side of the river and three weeks ago I sent 2 drays and 4 horses to cart them across but before they came back with the first load the punt sunk under a load of cattle and it is yet under water. I had the horses and drays for a fortnight on the other side, and they had to come home round by Nagambie. I am afraid I will be obliged to erect a punt to bring the rails across or I might not have them for a long time.'

On 20 May he reported—'I quite forgot to speak to you about the "secaters" the ones wanted are five (5) of the "*Forestier*

Geneve" the same as last year and five (5) of the ones with wire spring, and the outside of the handle cut like a file. There is no name upon them. With the two I have that will make a dozen.'

He added on 30 May, 'John Sullivan cannot work with the wire spring secaters he would like you to send six (6) more of the "Forestier Geneve".'

On 2 October 1878 he reported to his employer—

The ploughing of the vines is finished. It has been executed in 99½ days work instead of 117 days as in 1876; and 124½ days in 1877. I suppose this difference of time is due mostly to the difference of weather. The Digging will be all finished before the end of this week. I have begun to scarify, as the weeds are growing very fast. The vine also has begun growing fast and early; too early, because we had a very severe frost Thursday 26th September which did a great deal of harm in St. Andrews and St. Davids; but as it was very early and the vine yet very short it will grow again, and the crop might not be any the worse for it; only a little later. I have seen such a case in France.

I have begun the shearing on Monday last 30th September with three shearers. I expect to finish it, towards the end of next week, if all goes well. Very few of the lambs will be fit to shear, they are nearly all too young, some are just dropped and more are coming every day. The lambing season has been very long this year, it is not yet finished and there are more than two months since it began, we will have over three hundred.

I have given four (4) mares to 'Young Peer' at £3.15.0 each, the first half payable in January and the balance when the mare proves in foal. The four mares are 'Dido', 'Betsey', 'Burgundy', and 'Pearce's Cob'. The two last named and 'Topsey' are in foal by the 'Spaune'. I expect them to foal very shortly. I want to give 'Flower', 'Lucy' and 'Topsey' to a good draft horse, in order to get heavy foals for the plough and dray, but I have not as yet agreed for the price. I have made an offer, and I wait the answer every day.

41

Contrary to my expectations we have no flood at all since July, and I do not think that we will have any from the snow this year, because the snow has nearly all come down little by little, melted by the heat and light rain—We had only 4 days of rain during September and 1 inch and 10 points of water.

I hope you have remembered our need of two good grape mills, and a cellar pump during your visit to the Paris Exhibition. We want these three articles very badly.

In February 1880 he writes of improvements in hand—

The engine is already built in bricks on the other side of the yard where it looks a hundred times better than it did before and I am sure it will work far better too. When the day was a little cold and the wind from the south we could not get steam up. Now the harder it will blow the more steam it will make.

This year phylloxera attacked many vineyards but he says he 'can listen to others talk and be calm' and he notes remedies for this scourge—

The phylloxera is making an immense noise in the Colony just now. A French gentleman, at the request of the Victorian government, has inspected the Geelong vineyards; and has reported, that the insect of this colony was far more dangerous that the European one, being a great deal bigger, and much more vigorous, its destructive power was also much greater. Another commission of foreign competent men is to be invited by the government to reinspect the inspected district. All the papers are arguing on what should be done, and who should do it, but nobody seems inclined to do anything, except to ask the government to do the lot, or give them the money to do it with; as usual. It is every day the case, in this country, if their bed is not so soft, as they would like, they will ask the government to change the mattress, when it taxes them for the price, they begin to grumble. If however the government is to do everything, it must find the money to pay for the labour. They are now using lots of ink, paper, and time, to discuss the subject, but nobody does anything to stop the progress of the phylloxera. One of the writers on the subject says, that if the progress of the pest is not speedily checked, in ten years Victoria will have to import its wine. Those are not his words but the idea. So Chateau Tahbilk, is threatened, like all its Victorian brothers. This is a poor prospect, and would be very disheartening if there was no way to avoid the misfortune. But of all the Australian vineyards, yours is, without any doubt, the best able, if properly managed, to defy the terrible phylloxera. Of all the remedies Europe has tried the inundation is the most effective. This remedy, nature has provided for C.T. There is about 200 acres of ground which is generally flooded once or twice a year, and at times when the water would hurt nothing but the phylloxera. At least it has been so, for the last four years, which I have witnessed. There has been two floods a year, but always between vintage and the next blossoming, when the only harm it could do to the vineyard, would be to wet and enrich the soil, by the depot it leaves on its surface. If once in ten years, it should come at the blossoming season, and destroy the crop, the nine others would largely compensate for the lost one. European vignerons are also of the opinion that the phylloxera can do no harm in sandy soil, if it can live at all. As the half of St. Patrick's Paddock is of that nature, it would also be advisable to plant it. And for the same reason, the little Pigs Paddock, which extends from the pig yard to Hughes' cottage along the river. Some of it has been under vine already. It ought to be replanted as it is mostly sandy soil, and subject to flood. The Pigs Paddock near the lagoon, and the Flat Paddock which the lagoon surrounds ought, also, to be planted for this facility to be submerged. If ever the phylloxera reaches this vineyard, it is so thickly planted, and its soil so dry, that its destruction will only be a question of time, and the money buried in cellar and casks will then be a dead loss. . . . But by planting, at once, the ground above mentioned, we can look in the future with cheerful hearts; and with Victor Hugo, say (L'avenir! l'avenir! l'avenir c'est a moi! !). This is very doubtful if no immediate step is taken. I think this project, after due consideration, ought to be carried out at once, and plant the new vineyard with only 3 or 4 of the best kinds of vines, so as to command the market, when they come into bearing. If after the vineyard is established and producing, we should require artificial or prolonged floods, they could be very easily obtained by shutting the lagoon at its narrowest place. The whole expense would only amount to a few days labour, and the fixing of a door. If, after reflection, you think this project is worth carrying out, it can be started next winter. The lagoon Pigs Paddock is nearly cleared at the exception of a few dry trees, which could be rooted out for very little. And part of the Flat Paddock, could be cleared and planted at the same time.

There is no phylloxera in the vineyard yet there is no knowing when it might come. Prevention is better than cure. If the phylloxera was to destroy the old vineyard when the new one is in full bearing, you would not feel it much; but it would be very different, if the harm was done, when there would be no other vineyard to fall back upon.

In October 1881 de Coueslant describes a visit from Mr Hardy, owner of Tintara in South Australia.

I think he is about the largest wine, olives, almonds, and oranges and other fruits grower in South Australia. He got the Mayor's prize at the last Exhibition. In showing the place I asked his opinion about nearly everything. Of the cellar and wines he did not say anything worth repeating. But when we came to the vineyard he said 'If this vine was mine, I should root out every 2 rows upon 3 and in the one left I should root out every second vine; make it at best 12 by 8. I would go mad if I had to work this vine.' I have long expressed a similar opinion, [de Coueslant went on] but nothing has come of it although I did not propose to make the espace between the vines so wide. If the old vineyard had been

44

planted further apart it could be worked for a quarter of what it actually costs.

He also showed Mr Hardy his grape-mill about which he had already compained to Mr Bear and Mr Hardy agreed with him that it was too smooth. 'Make it rough with a cold chisel, it will work beautifully. But do not use it for grapes. . . . I should prefer to crush the grapes with the feet than using these mills. Not only do they make the work long and difficult, but being made of iron I think they injure the wine.'

However, de Coueslant received in June 1882 a grappoir bought by Mr Bear in France, which satisfied him. 'I think it will prove a very good instrument. It seems very simple and very complete. It will save a good bit of trouble besides economising four men at least.' On 15 July he went into detail on this.

The wine grower you met at London might not have known Guillot's egrappoir; I mean the one that you have bought. The first one I bought myself was also a Guillot's Egrappoir but a very different thing from the one you sent out. The one I bought and refused afterward, was a very primitive kind of machine, when the one I have received from you seems to me a very complete concern. Although I will have to make some modifications in it. But not in the mechanism, in the outside frame. It has been made to fit on the top of a fermenting vat, and we want it to travel along the floor. After that I think it will be a very effective machine. You, once before, said something about a platform, for the egrappoir, but did not give me any particulars. With the new egrappoir no platform will be wanted as it will throw the berries directly in the vat itself. My project for fixing the new presse room, is very similar to the one you describe in yours of 2nd June. Only instead of a travelling dish, the mill itself will travel from one vat to the other, and a tramway running along the middle of the floor will bring the grapes to it, carrying a full load at a time. If you refer to my letter of 27 April 1880, you will find that I have said something to you about the addition that I am now making at the end of the cellar. It consists of 40 feet of new building put over the 2 big vats. The vats as they were, were perfectly useless to the Company. I made a plan of the building which I thought wanted to cover the vats and showed it to Mr Browne, who approved of it, and now I am putting it up. My project is, when the building is up, to make a presse room of what they call the old stable, where the office used to be. To put there the presse and all the vats, if I can, and do there, and in the new building, all the fermenting, and pressing; and have the cellar itself as free as possible of vintage work. The grapes will be received by the end of the cellar instead of by the middle. And carry along the middle of the floor in tramway a full load at a time. As it is now it detains the drays standing too long at the door, when the grape pickers are standing in the vine waiting for them. I mean to have a dozen, or more, boxes than wanted to fit all the drays; so that when a dray is emptied it can take a new set of boxes and start at once; instead of waiting until its load is crushed. The boxes left by one dray will be emptied for the next. As to the solidarity of the building and bank on which it is built, I do not think that there is any fear, of either going with the flood. I will send you by next mail a plan and description of both.

This letter goes on—

I have tried to give you an idea, by the sketch herewith enclosed, of the addition I am now making to the end of the old cellar. The front of the lower part, is built of bricks but the remainder is wood; the end, the back and uper stories. The first story with its two large doors in the end is destined to receive the grapes in vintage. A double lift, worked with the same chains, will be fixed opposite the double door; fixed in such a way, that when one of the lifts will go up with a load of grapes, the other will come down with empty boxes; and be ready for the next dray coming in. The grapes will be carried from the door as I have mentioned, in my last letter. I think it will be far quicker than the present system. The second story will be used as a store room for oats. I have no place now, to put the oats wanted for the horses during the year. It used to be put in some of the cottages, but the cottages were not built for that purpose and they cannot stand it. The third story might be called an observation room; from which you will be able to have an eye all over the vineyard; which fact being known, might help the work a little. The uper floor tells its destination. As to the solidarity; when I started building I opened a trench all round for the foundations nearly 7 feet deep. Right down to the original old clay bank. And there I lay along the bottom of the trenches, on the hard ground, logs 18 inches square, all fixed one to the other by the end, and forming a frame of the shape and size of the building. The logs at the back, tied to the ones at the front, by other logs, going across the building, with both ends mortised and engaged, one end under the front, and the other under the back logs; so that one side cannot go unless the other follows. And I fixed all the uprights which formed the lower part of the building to that under ground frame and covered it up. So I do not think it can ever move. To secure the bank between the building and the river, I dug another trench along the foot of the bank, a little deeper than the one for the foundations; and I put (upright in it) logs of about 13 feet long, and from 1 foot diameter, upward; all touching each other, and standing about 6 feet over ground. I planted poplars outside of the logs; in the same trench at the same time. I then filled up the space between the building and those logs, or between the bank already formed and the logs, with the ground which came out from the new must tank; and planted over it all the couch grass that I could find through the vineyard. Now grass and poplars are growing and the bank is, I think, pretty secure at that place.

Irrigation he always considered important. In 1883 he stresses what it could mean to Chateau Tahbilk.

48

When Mr Thos Bear came here last, he mentioned the irrigation of the Vineyard. I strongly believe that, if I could have watered the vines last year (I mean for the 82 vintage) I could have augmented the crop by 20,000 gallons. And taken at 2/- only, it would have made some difference in the return. This season the vintage will be small, but if I could have given the vine a watering about the middle of December last, I could put 10,000 gallons more in the casks, than I will, this vintage. St. Patricks and St. Davids are very poor in grapes, as the frost was very severe in those two places; but the remainder of the vineyard had a very good crop (three months ago). But to day half of it is turned into raisins. But not sweet. It dries up, before it ripens. There seems to be no sap in the vine. Every year, since I am at Tahbilk, I have seen the crop perished for want of water. If the vineyard had been mine (supposing I had the money), I should have erected an engine and a pump long ago; and if I had had no money, I should have borrowed some for the purpose; because I strongly believe, that it would have paid me *one thousand per cent*. Besides augmenting the produce, it would have answered the purpose of early gathering, which you mention in yours of 11th January. The grapes, instead of filling, sweeten and dry up; and then give very little must but give it very rich. I have thought myself, long ago, that our wines might be improved in delicacy by gathering earlier, but will that be a recommendation for an English palate? English people accustomed to Port and Sherry, like strong wine. Although, probably, with time they will come to know better; but for the present they do not care for *light stuff*.

By 1890 fifty hogsheads a month were to be exported to London. Before he gave up his post as manager of Chateau Tahbilk, wines made under de Coueslant's guidance had won such awards at home and abroad as—

1881   Perth International Exhibition. A.F.L. & P. for Colonial Wines.
1881   Adelaide. Gold Medal for Colonial Wines.

1882	Societe Philomatique de Bordeaux, Exposition Universelle de Vins. Medaille de Progress.
1882	New Zealand, International Exhibition, Award for Australian Wines.
1883	Internationale Kolonial en Uitvoerhandel tentoonstelling. Amsterdam. Silver Medal.
1883-84	Calcutta International Exhibition. Chateau Tahbilk Wine.
1884	Victoria Intercolonial Exhibition of Wine, Grain Fruit, Etc. Award.
1884	The Smithers Gadd Cup for wine to Chateau Tahbilk.
1885	Melbourne, Champion Prize. Chateau Tahbilk Wine.
1886	Colonial & Indian Exhibition. London. Two Bronze Medals.
1886-87	The National Agricultural Society of Victoria.
	1st Prize. White Wine. Light Dry. 1886-87.
	1st Prize. White Wine. Full bodied sweet.
	1st Prize. Red Wine. Light Dry.
1887	Adelaide Jubilee International Exhibition. 1st Order of Merit.
1888	Melbourne. Centennial International Exhibition. Award of Honour.

3

Chateau Tahbilk

John Pinney Bear had been actively connected with Chateau Tahbilk for more than a quarter of a century. His had been the suggestion for use of the telegraph to hasten publication of advertisements for cuttings for the first plantings of vines in 1860. He had watched, if not directed, every step in the progress of farm and of vineyard from the clearing of timber on the river slopes, through the building of cellars and fermenting floor, the placing of presses and

vats, the buying of grape mills, farm stock, implements, rations, and seed for pastures and crops. His had been the final responsibility for financing operations of both farm and vineyard. He was not a trained vigneron or a farmer but he knew a good deal about running a farm, he had investigated vine-growing, wine-making and marketing abroad; and he had had considerable experience in business, in the buying and selling of stock and of station properties, of handling hired labour, of banking and of finance. Chateau Tahbilk had been the project into which he put most of his boundless energy and on which he spent much of his money, whatever else he had been interested in between 1841 and 1889, while Victoria grew from a handful of slab huts and other temporary dwellings set up on virgin land from the sea-coast to the Murray, to a well-settled independent State with its own dignified, solidly built capital city, its Legislative Assembly and Council—of which Mr Bear was a member for many years as he was a foundation member of St Peter's Eastern Hill, one of the city's finest churches.

As a boy of seventeen, about to leave for Australia, he had recorded in April 1841 in his journal 'about three o'clock to the Ship Tavern in Water Lane and had our dinner afterwards to some friends of Mr Duncan's wine-merchants went in their Vaults and had some wine'. When he returned from his last trip to London to die at Chateau Tahbilk on 27 October 1889, a man in his mid-sixties whose wines had won awards both in Australia and abroad and whose own 'Vaults' were to hold more prize-winning vintages, John Pinney Bear had proved that there was a market for the wines of the Goulburn abroad as well as in Victoria. He had also helped to create at Tabilk a little community, the unique flavour of which was to linger through the next quarter century. Francois de Coueslant was, of course, largely responsible for the building up of this community spirit during the years of his enlightened management and development of Chateau Tahbilk for the Bears. The letter-book shows his lively sense of dedication to his job, his intensely human interest in the welfare of his people, working on farm and in vineyard: his care for the progress of his vines, for the breeding of his work-horses—even for the quality of his bacon-pigs. He identified himself with life at the Chateau and in the surrounding district.

After de Coueslant's departure, and the death of John Pinney Bear, a period of partial neglect and failure was to be experienced at Chateau Tahbilk but, in the years immediately following 1889, the vineyard was producing large quantities of wine, and brandy of such quality that samples sent to Paris in 1893 by Joseph Gassies, a Frenchman appointed oenologist by William Wilson then resident manager, drew from the expert of the Moniteur Vinicole de Paris the report: 'Your brandy is of good quality, it has finesse, aroma, and a well pronounced wine taste and very agreeable.'

In February 1888, on the eve of John Pinney's last return to Tahbilk, Arthur Browne, secretary to the company, wrote from Melbourne to T. A. Rattray who had followed de Coueslant as manager at the vineyard:

'I am very sorry to hear that you estimate the vintage at only 60,000 gallons. Mr Bear will be greatly disappointed especially as I have told him that we purchased vats and casks in anticipation of a large yield.' Between that vintage and 1925 the vineyard's maximum year's production was to be 70,000 gallons; but, between 1911 and 1923, the maximum only once exceeded 40,000 gallons and it dropped to 14,265 in 1918, when mildew attacked the vines, and to 17,850 the year of a big flood.

The yield was 35,050 gallons in 1923 for 175 acres—the exact vineyard area—an average of about 200 gallons per acre. The vineyard was now more than sixty years old and it was suggested by Francois de Castella, then Victorian Government viticulturist, that this low yield was largely due to the absence of manuring. 'It is obviously unreasonable to expect continuance of productivity over a long series of years, without restitution in the shape of manure, of the plant food removed annually by the crops. . . . Manuring on a generous scale should considerably increase the yield. It should be applied fairly deep and a couple of years would probably elapse before any result could be expected. . . . I am also of the opinion that marked improvement could be achieved by a system of winter irrigation, especially in dry winters.'

We know that de Coueslant urged Mr Bear to agree to spend money on irrigation but little seems to have been done to develop Chateau Tahbilk's resources during the first quarter of the twentieth century. After 1890 management of farm and of vineyard was in the hands of William Wilson—recommended to Bear's executors by de Castella—and later of his son, John Wilson.

Mrs Bear and her daughters continued to live in London and, until her death there in 1925 at the age of 92, she corresponded at great length with John Wilson on methods of management. But an absentee owner, particularly one who has not had practical experience of management, is not always able to direct successfully a business which, like Chateau Tahbilk, requires special understanding of seasonal needs. After Mrs Bear's death the estate was put on the market and bought by the late Reginald Purbrick, M.P., father of the present owner.

By June 1929 the area of the vineyard had fallen to 115 acres of which 75 acres were old vines, 17 acres replanted in 1927 (12 acres of Uni-Blanc or White Hermitage and 5 of Marsanne), 12 acres replanted in 1928 with resistants stock to be field grafted and 11 acres with grafted rootlings. The total yield for four *years* had been 47,400 gallons, the lowest vintage being 1927 with 7,000 gallons, following a series of disastrous frosts, and the highest vintage in 1929 with 18,400 gallons.

Making a new report so that the Purbricks might consider what could be done in the future with their vineyard, de Castella insisted 'Chateau Tahbilk has in the past been a productive and profitable vineyard property and can be so again. The soil and climate are admirably suited for the vine and I do not think any other form of cultivation could show the results the vine is capable of on the vineyard portion of the estate.' 'Tahbilk,' he went on, 'is very well suited for the production of a class of wine that is becoming less plentiful

Eric S. Purbrick

in Australia as time goes on. I refer to light table wines of Claret and Chablis or Hock types, which the vineyard has in the past produced in quantity and of a satisfactory standard. Such wines are less expensive to make than sweet wines, as no spirit is needed for their fortification. The demand for them is increasing, owing to the recent abandonment of many of those vineyards in the cooler districts best capable of producing them. The recent expansion in Australian wines has been in sweet wines. Light dry wines are thus becoming scarcer and more sought after, a tendency which will become more accentuated as time goes on.'

De Castella then strongly advised deep and early winter ploughing, manuring, improved cultivators for spring and summer working

57

of the soil and, again, winter irrigation (de Coueslant's constant desire during his Tahbilk days); as well as the replacement of small unsatisfactory areas with vines grafted on resistant stocks. He pointed out that Chateau Tahbilk, like many Victorian vineyards, had suffered heavily from phylloxera in the last years of the nineteenth century, when many vineyards were partially or even totally destroyed by this insect attacking the vines.

Many vines on Tahbilk were killed by the disease—of those left 'the vines have survived the insect in a truly remarkable manner owing to the sandy nature of the sub-soil', so that the best portions of the old vineyard 'are not suffering at all from the presence of the insect but certain parts where the soil is stiffer—as it is on the Riesling block—are depressed and the yield is reduced in consequence'. He told Eric Purbrick when he took over the management of Chateau Tahbilk that his land wanted more iron in it—the metal kind which comes behind horses.

This excellent advice from a member of the wine-growing family which had been associated with the fortunes of Chateau Tahbilk in a friendly way since the birth of the vineyard was to be followed by Eric Purbrick. For the new owner the first problems were to replenish the vine-stocks and to provide modern machinery for dealing with cultivation and vintage.

When he took on the task of rehabilitating the estate Eric Purbrick was twenty-eight. Born in Sydney, he grew up in Melbourne, went to England with his family in 1921, studied law and history at Jesus College, Cambridge, graduating in 1925. He first visited Tahbilk after his father bought the property that year. Back in England in 1929 he was called to the Bar and spent some of his spare time in winter mountaineering in Switzerland.

At first glance his background and training would not appear to have fitted him particularly for his work at Chateau Tahbilk; and when he began his task in 1931 Australia was in the midst of the economic depression which affected business all over the civilised world. Like Charles Joseph Latrobe he was a man of varied interests,

58

a person with definite tastes and plenty of vitality, able to learn quickly, to sense the atmosphere of his inheritance, to rebuild its past as well as to plan for its future.

He had visited the Black Forest in Germany in 1928 and been fascinated by a wrought-iron sign, going back to 1732, which he saw hanging outside a weinhaus. A copy of this was made with the words 'Chateau Tahbilk' round the sign to use as a distinctive trademark for his vineyard. Wine bottled at Chateau Tahbilk bears a printed replica of the large sign which now hangs above the main entrance to the cellars, a sign which has merged as naturally with its background as has its owner. For Eric Purbrick has not only concentrated on wine-making but has re-established and re-interpreted the spirit of Chateau Tahbilk as expressed in the community grouped round the vineyard and in the re-organised cellars. Visitors to Tabilk vineyards almost a hundred years ago were fascinated by the lay-out of the cellars, the workmen's stone cottages near the orchard, the homestead nestling in its surrounding gardens. After the building of the Goulburn Weir, when a portion of Chateau Tahbilk was taken over by the Water Commission, a long wooden bridge was built to give direct access from the vineyard area, across a wide backwater of the Goulburn, to the homestead settlement and the cellars. Visitors who come now to Chateau Tahbilk in autumn, at the time of the vintage, will not meet a horde of itinerant pickers with nothing more than the seasonal worker's interest in a casual job, but men and women who have been living and working at the Chateau with their families for years, contributing in their own particular way in vineyard or in cellar towards the enterprise that is Chateau Tahbilk in 1960.

But, to begin with, there were the twin problems of production and marketing for the new owner to face; and always there was the river for good or for ill.

Flood came again to Tahbilk in 1934, the river rising until water flowed into the cellars and the vineyard was covered. The replanting programme had been begun in 1927, the 'iron' needed was gradually

59

being provided in the form of new machinery for cultivating the vines but Eric Purbrick's most urgent need that year was customers for his wine. So he began a series of runs in his utility wagon up and down the Goulburn valley and elsewhere, to sell kegs of wine to local hotelkeepers. Every vintage that had quality was kept back to mature before marketing. When he took over only bulk sales of wine were being made. Immediately after World War II he began to work out a programme for the development of bottled wine sales and to appoint agents in the various Australian States. Export in bulk to the United Kingdom, which had reached 50 hogsheads a month in 1890, was to begin again; but not until 1952.

The old homestead, picturesque as it looks in the photographs taken in John Pinney Bear's day, was much worn by time and by weather. In 1936 it was pulled down. The new one, which rose from the original foundations, preserves the nineteenth century atmosphere, heightened by its surrounding ever-green lawns and tree-shadowed gardens, by the paved courtyard and the overgrown grape-arbour leading onto the cellar yard, bounded on its outer edge by the building known locally as 'the church'—so used when it was the only place large enough to hold the Chateau Tahbilk community and others in the district who wished to worship with them. As far as possible the new homestead re-interpreted the old. One room overlooking the Goulburn was actually preserved in the rebuilding and some timber from the old cellars was used inside the house, as well.

Scarcely had the new homestead been completed and filled with the owner's treasured possessions from all parts of the world when war broke out in 1939 and Eric Purbrick enlisted. His war-service was followed by a year in Greece with an Australian Red Cross unit and he was not able to continue his work at Chateau Tahbilk until 1946.

On 12 July 1947 a curiously interesting ceremony took place in the 'new' cellar at Tahbilk when John Pinney Bear's 1876 cache was opened and the wine he had sealed up when laying the cornerstone with his silver trowel was rediscovered in the presence of a number of 'wine' men, including Francois de Castella, the Seabrooks and others who from their superior knowledge had helped a new owner to learn how to run his vineyard. After being buried for seventy years inside the cellar wall, the red Tahbilk was drinkable but the white had suffered from the effects of time. The bottles are to be replaced by two of 1960 vintage and the cache resealed to celebrate the vineyard's centenary.

Since 1947 the reputation of Chateau Tahbilk has been steadily re-established. Now the estate covers 2,800 acres of the rich river-flats, 100 of these being in vines which produce up to 40,000 gallons a year, some from the ten acres of original roots which resisted the phylloxera and, after a hundred years of life, still bear good wine grapes. In the cellar area, which covers one acre, all wine-making processes go on under one roof, where red wine is matured in wood for up to two years and white for eight months but where electrically driven machinery and plastic hosing have replaced the primitive steam-driven engine, belts and hoses and the nineteenth century French grape-mills of de Coueslant's day, where automatic corking and sealing machines deal with the wines selected for bottle sales to New Guinea, New Zealand, Fiji, Malaya, Hong Kong and Manila, as well as in Australia.

The farm, always an important section of Chateau Tahbilk, is now run by John Purbrick who joined his father in 1955 after practical experience of jackerooing in the Riverina and elsewhere. The farmland which is his responsibility now carries 2,700 crossbred ewes for the breeding of lambs, as well as 500 dry sheep and 150 beef cattle—Shorthorns and Herefords; 200 acres are under lucerne which is cut for hay or green fodder. Rye and subterranean clover have been planted and the pastures sown largely with phalaris tuberosa. Use is now made of spray irrigation. The story ends, as it began, with the river.

·　·　·　·　·

When Anthony Trollope, one of the most prolific and popular of nineteenth century novelists, returned from a trip to Australia in the last decade of the nineteenth century and published his impressions of the trip, R. H. Horne, who had been living in England since 1869, felt impelled, on reading these, to comment particularly on Trollope's remarks about Australian wines. Thinking back to his Tabilk experiences he wrote:

Riesling, Cawarra, Kaludah (the pale or the Rosie Kaludah), the red Hermitage, the Shiraz—the exquisite flori-vinous bouquet of some of the Australian wines, especially the pale straw-coloured, or light golden-tinted wines, probably the taste for them has to be acquired. . . . Some of the Victorian wines have been almost as luscious as a liqueur, yet without any sugar having been added. What then must be the extraordinary inherent qualities of the grapes that shall be so sweet entirely from their own saccharine properties, or so heady from their natural alcohol? Here is a foundation for future vignerons to work upon. Here are the elements and the means for the production of wines, which in process of no distant time, will rival the finest wines of the old Continent—that will cure the labouring classes of their habitual drunkenness, as Mr Trollope does, I think, foresee—and that will as surely supersede more than half the wine of the old countries now drunk in England as the Australian and New Zealand pre-served meats will bring down the price of Butchers' meat pro-duced in the United Kingdom.

Could Horne have foreseen the choice of a 'light golden-tinted' Tahbilk Chablis for drinking at an official luncheon given to Her Majesty Queen Elizabeth II, by the Commonwealth Parliamentary Association at Westminster Hall on 27 May 1953, how delighted he would have been with the result of his labours 'to establish a vine-yard on the banks of the Goulburn'. And how it would appeal to the scientific side of his imagination if he knew that 20,000 feet above ground travellers dining on jet planes of the Trans-Australia

Airlines may drink Tahbilk wines from miniature bottles; while pilots who are familiar with the contours of the Goulburn valley can distinguish, as their aircraft pass over Mangalore, a faint outline below which they recognise as the Major's Line.

PART TWO

CHATEAU TAHBILK
GROWS UP

4

The Sixties

The grape vine is not indigenous to Australia, having been first planted in this country by Captain Arthur Phillip who brought rootlings with the First Fleet in 1788. Given the fact then, that wine-making on a commercial scale did not commence until the 1820s there are only a few contemporary vineyards and wineries which are a century old and fewer still which are a quarter of the way into their second hundred years. But with 1985, Tahbilk became one of this select handful and achieved the 125th year of its active life. Indeed, as the visitor approaching the property for the first time and entering its confines by way of the wooden bridge which spans the lagoon will note there are still vines—a few rows of Shiraz—which were planted in 1860. They are still bearing fruit, a circumstance believed to be unique in an Australian vineyard.

The attainment of Tahbilk's 125th birthday gave Eric Purbrick much with which to occupy his mind. It provided an opportunity to reflect with satisfaction on the 60 years of Purbrick ownership of the gracious and picturesque 'Tabilk run' and on the 54 years that had passed since he himself became its owner. At the same time, he found himself in the happy position of being able to contemplate the past with satisfaction and to look with optimism to the future of the vineyard.

Among his pleasant memories was the day of September 24, 1960 —when he and his family gave an anniversary luncheon to about 200 guests.

This marked Chateau Tahbilk's Centenary, the account of which is covered in Part 1 which Enid Moodie Heddle wrote at the invitation of Eric Purbrick and copies of which were presented to friends of the vineyard on that occasion. Among those present were four generations of Purbricks—Mrs Dorothy Purbrick, Eric's mother, Eric himself, his son John and John's two eldest children, Alister and Deborah. The then Prime Minister of Australia Mr (later Sir) Robert Menzies and his wife Dame Pattie attended, as did Deputy Prime Minister, (later Sir John) McEwen and Dame Ann McEwen. The chairman of the National Trust, Sir Daryl Lindsay, and Lady Lindsay were there, as was Mr Ian Seppelt, over from Adelaide as chairman of the Australian Wine Board, his cousin Robert Seppelt, President of the Federal Viticultural Council of Australia, and acknowledged wine enthusiast Mr James MacDonald, M.L.A., representing the Premier of Victoria.

Although September 24, 1960 was a wet wintry day, there was joy and happiness in the air with no rigid formality at this luncheon. There was a toast by Ian Seppelt to the future of Chateau Tahbilk, a suitable response by Eric Purbrick and that was sufficient. After lunch the party crossed to the cellars—the old cellars, naturally—

where the famed Menzies wit flowed as easily and as unrestrainedly as the Tahbilk wine. The Prime Minister, at Eric Purbrick's request, carried on a tradition begun by John Pinney Bear in 1876. Behind a niche in the cellar wall he placed two bottles of Tahbilk wine of the year's vintage—a Reisling and a Shiraz—saying as he did: 'I have great pleasure in depriving the people of Australia of this wine for 100 years when none of you will be here and, what is worse, neither shall I.' With them went an instruction that they were not to be disturbed for one hundred years.

What, one wonders from a vantage point 25 years later, lies ahead for some future Purbrick as he and his guests assemble around that same niche—it is identified by a plaque at the main entrance to the cellars—on September 24, 2060? Will the robust Shiraz have enjoyed its century of life and seen it out in reasonable health? Will the more delicate Riesling have found the years too much for it?

Mark Purbrick, Eric's younger grandson (brother of Alister), was not born at the time of the Centenary Luncheon but, at the opening of the two Tahbilk Wines in 2060 will, with any good fortune, be 99 years and 11 months!

That day, too, Sir Daryl Lindsay unveiled the National Trust's tribute to Chateau Tahbilk in which it gave it suitable recognition as being 'among highly significant examples of early rural architecture worthy of preservation.'

On October 5, a few days later Sydney Fells, chairman of John E. Fells & Sons Ltd., who have been agents in Britain for Chateau Tahbilk since 1952, gave a luncheon at his company's London Bridge cellars to honour Chateau Tahbilk's Centenary.

At this lunch the guest of honor was Sir Eric Harrison, K.C.V.O., the High Commissioner for Australia, while others present included Col. Sir William Leggatt, Agent General for Victoria (who had practised as a solicitor near Tahbilk in 1922), Harold Morris, the Australian Wine Board's representative in the United Kingdom, Board members Ron Haselgrove and John Guinand who were visiting London, Sir Rupert de la Bere, a former Lord Mayor of London who had done much to promote Australian wines during his term of office, John Burgoyne, wine writers Raymond Postgate, Vyvyan Holland and the French-born Anglophile founder of the Wine and Food Society Andre Simon, F. F. Cockburn, President of the London Wine Club, James Chaplin, chairman of the Australian company Emu Wines, J. R. Denny, Master of the Vintners Company and the 21-year-old Peter Dechaineux, Eric Purbrick's stepson who, as a Sub Lieutenant in the Royal Australian Navy, had come up from Plymouth for the occasion.

In his speech, Sir Eric Harrison paid tribute to the progress being made by Australian wines and to Chateau Tahbilk and then congratulated Mr Purbrick by telephone, the proprietor of Tahbilk having put a long-distant call (rare in those days) from Australia.

Mr Purbrick had arranged a special parcel of Tahbilk wines for the luncheon, which included the 1959 Riesling which had just taken first prize at the Sydney show, the 1954 Shiraz and a special bottling of the 1958 Cabernet Sauvignon.

So it was that, in an atmosphere of peace and gaiety, the 100-year-old Chateau Tahbilk celebrated the end of its first century and entered the long march into another.

. . . . .

It is as well in any study of the history of Tahbilk to bear in mind something of the state of the Australian wine industry and the country's way of life at the beginning of the nineteen sixties. The enormous changes in our lifestyle during the post war years following 1946 had barely begun in 1960.

Total wine produced throughout the country in the first year of the new decade amounted to a paltry 153 million litres (by comparison with today's mark of close to 400 million) and Australians, already among the world's foremost beer consumers, drank about one litre each of wine a year (as against today's figure of 20 litres).

70

John Purbrick

Such wine as was drunk was mostly fortified and five o'clock sherry parties were a popular nation-wide form of entertainment.

But Eric Purbrick, encouraged by Francois de Castella, the Victorian Government's Viticulturalist of the time, placed his (and Tahbilk's) faith in table wines, white and red, both of which, in the manner of time, were still fermented in wooden vats. More and more, Purbrick explored other and more rewarding avenues, travelling regularly to Britain, the Middle East and parts of Asia to consolidate his already-established markets and to open new agencies.

71

The patterns of Australian living after 1960, that were largely changed due to the influx of migrants from Europe and Asia, also bought about radical changes at Tahbilk.

Gone were the days when Eric Purbrick had to tour the countryside in an old utility truck doing his best to sell his wine to hotels and wine saloons. Instead, more and more he—and a small on-the-spot sales staff—dealt with wine enthusiasts who came to him rather than he going to them. Tahbilk in those years, well before the rebirth of the Yarra Valley, was the closest vineyard and winery to Melbourne and people flocked to the picturesque cellars to buy and, in doing so, to learn about wine for these were the years when wine tastings and wine classes were at their most popular and books on wine proliferated on booksellers' shelves almost as much as did cookery books. The day of the now-ubiquitous wine 'cask' had not arrived and home bottling was at its height with Tahbilk, like other wineries around the country, selling large quantities of wine in bulk, putting it either into containers the customers had brought with them (in some instances, disused beer barrels) or in plastic receptacles of various measures. More and more, too, both Eric Purbrick, his son John and certain members of the staff found themselves being looked upon as founts of knowledge as people found that one of the very best ways to learn about wine was (and is) to discuss it with the man who had made it. Much of Tahbilk—the century-old cellars, the huge vats and casks and other appurtenances of a winemaker's craft—remained the same but there was an almost-contrast atmosphere of excitement and jollity about the place which it had not known before, certainly not in Eric Purbrick's time.

As the Sixties progressed, the planting programme increased in the face of added demand for Tahbilk's whites and reds. The most popular wine styles—Cabernet Sauvignon, Shiraz, Marsanne and Riesling—saw extra area under vine for the respective grape varieties needed and further extensions and remodelling were carried out to the fermenting cellars.

It was during this period, too, that both Eric and John Purbrick experienced two separate pleasures, both of them dear to their hearts. John had taken up flying as a pastime and, in due course, was granted a permit to carry passengers. During his days of flying alone, his had been the first eyes to see Chateau Tahbilk in its entirety—the vineyards, the cellars, the Church, the homestead, the land not given to the vine, the Goulburn on which it nestled, the lagoons that dot it. As soon as the opportunity arose, he took his father aloft to experience the same unrestrained joy and thrill. One can only speculate on what would have gone through Eric Purbrick's mind at the time for, spread out below him was the scene of his unceasing labours, of his triumph in the face of adversity, the core of his hopes, and the home he had built in a style close to the original. It lay there to delight his eye and his heart—this peaceful part of Australia which was his. But his mind must have turned, too, to so many who had preceded him in the days of Tahbilk's struggle for existence and he must have known, deep within him, that it had all been worthwhile.

The second thing to bring great joy to father and son was the declaration by Alister then, like his father and grandfather before him, at Melbourne Grammar School, that he had conquered that distressing period in any teenage boy of not knowing 'what I want to be when I grow up'. He wanted, he told them, to be a winemaker and to Eric particularly, who had handled both aspects of Tahbilk's activities—viticultural and pastoral—since he had arrived there in 1931 but who had increasingly left the latter side to John since his son had joined him in 1955, Alister's welcome decision meant much more than might have appeared on the surface. Eric Purbrick knew that, in time and if all went according to plan, Tahbilk would have a fully qualified winemaker for the first time. By arrangement with Alister's headmaster, the boy's school curriculum was altered slightly to cater for the further new aim in his life.

For some time, Eric and Mary Purbrick had staged occasional dinners for the Australian members of the Confrerie des Chevaliers du Tastevin, a France-based group of wine lovers of which he—as

Mary was later to become—was a Chevalier. In 1969, Tahbilk was appointed to be the spiritual home in this country of the body whose avowed purpose is to know and to love the wine of Burgundy. A plaque in the homestead proudly proclaims this fact of which the Australian-born winemaker and dedicated wine-enthusiast is justifiably proud.

Alister Purbrick

74

5

The Seventies

The Seventies, destined in several ways to be memorable in the history of Tahbilk, began auspiciously with yet another presentation of Chateau Tahbilk Cabernet Sauvignon to the Queen during her visit to Australia in 1970. The following year emerged as a classic vintage year at Tahbilk, especially for its Cabernet Sauvignon which Robin Bradley, in the first edition of his book *Australian Wine Vintages*, awarded a maximum of seven points in his assessment of quality, recommending that it would reach its peak of drinking pleasure in the year 1995. The same high approval was to be accorded twice again in the decade—in 1978 and 1979. In the same year, bottle storage was enlarged to hold a further 25,000 dozen while at the same time extension to the cellars allowed for oak maturation of an additional 54,000 litres.

In 1972, dealing with considerably less area under vine than preprevails now in 1985, pickers—Tahbilk still retains the old-fashioned but tried-and-true method of employing human labour to reap the harvest—brought in a record (in quantity) crop, sufficient to yield close to 450,000 litres, double the average of other years. Their reward was a surprise turn to the annual picnic which formerly had been held on the property. Instead they were taken by train to Echuca, then by paddle steamer up-stream to a pre-arranged (by John) landing spot where a happy picnic was held on the banks of the river. Some wine from that record vintage was to achieve an unusual fame of its own.

Some time later cellar hands, engaged in pumping wine from one cask to another, realised midway through the exercise that, for the first time in living memory, Cabernet Sauvignon was being blended with Shiraz—a mishap which was to have a permanent result. When the wine, the 1972 Chateau Tahbilk Cabernet-Shiraz, was shown at the first-ever Expovin wine exhibition in Melbourne in 1976, it was greeted with much enthusiasm, so much so that it continues to be an annual practice at Tahbilk to blend a certain amount of the two wine styles which had first come together by an unforeseen human error. However, as lovers of Tahbilk wine realise only too well, the two varieties are also still bottled separately.

1973 saw an addition to the buildings that constitute Chateau Tahbilk, an event which had not occurred for many years, so that it was only natural that the person responsible—Eric Purbrick himself, who that year had entered his own seventies—should lay the foundation stone. This was the store, quickly dubbed 'The Cathedral' because of its architectural style, which stands at the far end of the original cellars, adjacent to the three-tiered tower. The planners and builders successfully overcame two difficulties they avoided any tendency towards modern design and resisted as well any temptation to fake antique.

In March of that year, during vintage, Tahbilk was honoured by a visit from a member of the Royal Family—His Royal Highness Prince Philip, Duke of Edinburgh. After an inspection of the premises guided by the senior Purbrick, he and his entourage were given a buffet luncheon during the course of which John Purbrick, in charge of the dispensing of wine for the meal, committed a *faux pas* which has been treasured as a 'family boo-boo' ever since.

He asked 'Your Royal Highness, would you prefer a Rosé, white or red wine?'

'Thank you,' the Prince replied, 'but I'm not much of a red wine man. I'll have a glass of white.'

Having provided him with a glass, John made to pour from a bottle of Chateau Tahbilk Marsanne at which the Prince, with a wry smile, said: 'I think you'll find that it'll pour better if you take the cork out.'

76

On a glorious November day in 1975, Tahbilk passed another milestone when the 'New Cellars', those underneath The Church (so named because it was the scene in years gone by for religious service to be held there by the local clergyman for residents of the surrounding district), recorded their centenary. The Purbrick family gave an alfresco luncheon to guests assembled in the garden of the homestead after which the Federal Parliamentarian, Mr Tony Street, deputising that day for the soon-to-be Prime Minister, Mr Malcolm Fraser, unveiled the plaque which commemorates the occasion. (It should be mentioned that Mr Fraser did later visit Tahbilk and 'make the token gesture' commemorated by his name.) A little afterwards, The Victorian Government's Minister for State Development and Tourism, Mr Murray Byrne, laid the foundation stone of the George Comi Cellars opposite The Church, named for Tahbilk's long-time senior employee who had been associated with Eric Purbrick since 1936. It was that afternoon, too, when the young Alister Purbrick, only just recently having attained his majority, made a speech of thanks which so impressed Mr Street that he suggested—quite seriously—that the young man should enter politics.

By this time, Tahbilk had been joined in the Goulburn Valley by the first of his (now half-dozen) winemaking neighbours. This was Mitchelton which stands on the opposite bank of the Goulburn River and which was as futuristic in design and concept as Tahbilk is picturesque and 'old world'.

In the true spirit of country people and of wine-minded people in particular, Eric Purbrick had unstintingly made available cuttings from his vines, especially Marsanne, hitherto almost exclusively his property to the new vignerons. In spite of predictions at the time that the newcomer would adversely affect the way of life of the old hand, Tahbilk cellar door sales jumped noticeably as visitors to Mitchelton took the opportunity to knock on an older door. Today, a happy relationship exists between the two wineries, especially between Alister Purbrick, winemaker at Tahbilk and Don

Lewis and David Treager winemakers of Mitchelton.

The latter years of the Nineteen Seventies were tinged with both joy and concern for the Purbrick's and Tahbilk. Alister had gone to study oenology at the Roseworthy Agricultural College in South Australia in 1972 and had graduated in 1975. To gain experience of practical winemaking, he worked the 1976 and 1977 vintages at Coonawarra in South Australia with the Mildara Wine Company and then returned to Tahbilk to handle the 1978 vintage with his father and grandfather, the latter still very much in charge of the winemaking. This meant that, for the first time, three generations of Purbricks had been simultaneously involved in one vintage. But that same year brought some worry to Eric Purbrick and his vineyard workers when *Phylloxera vastatrix*, the louse which had done so much harm to the vineyards of Victoria last century, reappeared at Tahbilk.

Originally phylloxera made its entry into Australia at Geelong, thought to have been brought in on a consignment of vine cuttings from France. In November 1877 Mr H. King, of the Fairview nursery at Fyansford, first noticed that a couple of his vines were not doing well. Investigation led him to believe that only they were affected but within six months his whole vineyard had to be uprooted, so thoroughly had the pests done their tragic work.

It is thought to have reached Tahbilk in its inexorable and destructive march to the north-east of the State, wiping out scores of properties on the way about 1899. So drastically did it strike that it left untouched only 55 hectares which had been planted on moist, sandy soil that had evidently protected the vines from the disease. All of the 55 hectares has since been pulled out save seven rows of the original Shiraz, planted in 1860 which are now identified by a signpost and which are still productive, with wine from their fruit being bottled separately.

Phylloxera's second appearance at Tahbilk was noted late in 1978 and by March 1979 most of the vines where it was found on the roots were showing signs of being weak and within 12 months were of little or no commercial value. The vines were becoming infested in one season, showing themselves as weak in the second and then declining rapidly in the third.

That section of the vineyard affected by the disease was known as the Plains Vineyard and at the time of its being planted to Riesling, Shiraz and Cabernet Sauvignon in a programme that began in 1975, it was not known that there still existed a problem with phylloxera at Tahbilk. Up-rooting began almost immediately after phylloxera was discovered and in 1982 a programme of re-planting on phylloxera-resistant stock was begun with expectations that it will be complete by 1987. The area to be replanted by that year will be 22 hectares consisting of 10 hectares of Cabernet Sauvignon, six of Riesling, three of Semillon, two of Sauvignon Blanc and one of Cabernet Franc, bringing it back to the original area size. In 1985 a small amount of fruit was picked from the replanted area.

1979 was also the year when Alister took over the winemaking reins full-time, giving rise to his grandfather's remark that 'at last, Tahbilk has a fully qualified winemaker'. His first vintage was not without event.

In the light of his professional training, abetted by the seemingly ceaseless demand by the wine-drinking public for white wines, both he and his grandfather knew that it was inevitable Tahbilk would have to modernise much of its equipment. Although Alister was (and is) quite determined to make Tahbilk red wines in the time-honoured way of fermentation in open vats with maturation in aged oak, he was equally convinced that something different was needed for whites if they were to be produced in the accepted modern delicate style.

So he was given funds to cover the purchase of much needed stainless steel equipment for both winemaking and storage, to be installed (it was hoped) for the 1979 vintage. But grapes, like any fruit, wait for no man. Despite this and other unexpected happen-ings—such as the steel catwalk being installed six inches out of

plumb and unwanted rain dousing both staff and fruit since the roofing of the new building was not complete when vintage began— Alister made his first vintage solo at Tahbilk in what can only be described as unfortunate circumstances. But he succeeded so remarkably, that with the first wine he ever entered in an Australian wine show—the 1979 Chateau Tahbilk Semillon at that year's Brisbane show—he won a Gold Medal, a feat which was likened

at the time as being somewhat akin to a batsman making a century in his first Test match. Furthermore, he repeated the felicitous achievement by taking out another Gold Medal at the 1979 Perth Royal Show, this time for a Rhine Riesling. The family pride on both occasions (when everyone concerned was only too conscious of the difficulties encountered in making the wines) was great. By the time the excellent new white wine fermentation cellars were eventually complete they were of such modernity that they allowed for successive vintages to be handled by one—at most, two men and for the storage of more than 300 000 litres of wine. Now the 125-year-old winery and its accompanying installations are geared to handle 1000 tonnes of fruit a year though, in the present circumstances, it has an average production of between 500 and 650 tonnes, equivalent to 340 000 to 400 000 litres. It is truly in miniature, one of the best organised and most efficient wineries in the country.

New plans and a bold move to tackle the New South Wales wine market more strongly led John Purbrick to move to Sydney in early 1979 and within a comparatively short time had so succeeded that sales of Tahbilk wines there had multiplied threefold.

6

The Eighties

In 1981—a fully-automatic bottling line was installed, something hidden (as a rule) from the visiting public but, to those who appreciated the need for top-quality behind-the-scenes activity as beneficial an acquisition as Tahbilk could buy. In the same year George Comi (after whom, as has been seen, the Purbrick family happily named its newest cellars) suffered a severe illness from which, happily he has now recovered. Although it forced him to retire, he still lives on the property, as does his son Bernie who is still in Tahbilk employ.

George Comi first came to Chateau Tahbilk in 1936 as a lad, working as a general hand on the property before beginning his training in wine in the vineyards and as a cellar hand. On his return from World War 2 he came back to work again for Eric Purbrick, rising to become vineyard foreman and, about 1955, cellar manager and winemaker. On his retirement he had given 45 years' service to Tahbilk and Eric had learned during that time to value his deep love for wine, his adept making, and his sound knowledge of it—as, indeed do members of the industry throughout the country who know him.

After some agitation by winemakers and the general public, the Victorian Government legislated for Sunday trading in April, 1981 and, after a delay in operating (Eric Purbrick at first was against it but later admitted a misjudgment), Tahbilk opened for cellar door sales on Sunday between the hours of noon and five o'clock in the afternoon. This would have been instrumental in seeing the number of visitors rise to an annual figure of between 50000 and 60000.

In 1983 yet another member of the Royal Family drank Tahbilk wine—so far is known, for the first time. It was served to the Prince of Wales during his—and the Princess'—visit to this country. In any event, there is hope that in 20 or 25 years' time Alister will be asked to make arrangements for some Tahbilk wine to be put before Prince William or Prince Harry, sons of the heir to the Throne.

At this stage as Tahbilk ends its fifth quarter of a century and embarks on another, there are ten classic varieties of grapes planted on its 81 hectares—Shiraz, Cabernet Sauvignon, Cabernet Franc for red wines and Marsanne, Riesling, White Hermitage, Semillon, Chardonnay, Chenin Blanc and Sauvignon Blanc for whites, but, as demand locally, interstate and overseas increases there seems no reason why that number should not be added to.

But not only area under vine has increased since Enid Moodie

Heddle wrote the history of Tahbilk's first century. With the acquisition of the Cathedral, the George Comi cellars and the new White Fermenting cellar in the intervening years, storage in wood and in stainless steel now amounts to 827 411 litres while there is capacity to accommodate 100 000 dozen.

One of the newer features of Chateau Tahbilk—modern in concept yet very much designed to keep its past in perspective—is the allocation of a small area at the end of the original cellars closest to the homestead for use as a museum. There, old winery and wine-making equipment of various kinds, old photographs and memorabilia are on display, attracting those winelovers who are sensitive of Tahbilk's history.

Yet amid this emphasis on wine (this book, after all, is the history of an Australian vineyard) sight should not be lost of the fact that the 'Tahbilk run' is still in operation and that part of it not given to the vine is devoted to other pursuits such as cropping and agistment for both sheep and cattle.

All in all, Chateau Tahbilk remains the same quiet and tranquil haven that it has been throughout the 125 years of its life. Only at vintage time during March, April and May is the restful atmosphere of the countryside disturbed by the feverish activity necessary to bring the ripe grapes to the crusher and fermenters, there to let nature (assisted a little by man) reveal what she can do so ably—turn the fruit of the vine into that marvellous liquid that has been known and loved for a century and a quarter as the wine of Chateau Tahbilk.

· · · · ·

The Purbrick family have seen changes and developments in their home as is natural in all small communities. Since the Centenary Luncheon in 1960, of the youngest there on that day, Alister is now, winemaker at Chateau Tahbilk. He is also managing director of the family company, Tahbilk Proprietary Ltd. In his time at Chateau Tahbilk, he has found time to devote his energy to both wine industry matters outside his immediate concern and to sporting endeavours in the neighbouring township of Nagambie. He, like his grandfather (who is an honorary life member) is a member of the prestigious Viticultural Society of Victoria and also of the Melbourne Club.

In October, 1982 he married Rosa Dal Farra appropriately for a Purbrick, in the 'Church' on the property, which stands above ground, over the 'New Cellars' of 1875. His sister Deborah, too, is married, again providing, as a Purbrick, an appropriate touch in her choice of partner. Her husband is Allan George and they live in the Upper Hunter Valley of New South Wales where he is a wine-maker with Rosemount Wines. Both Rosa and Deborah, in that order, presented their husbands with daughters—and thus John with grandchildren and Eric with great-grandchildren—in 1984.

Mark, youngest of John's children and not born at the time of Tahbilk's Centenary luncheon, is now managing the Royal Mail Hotel in Nagambie which Tahbilk Proprietary Ltd. purchased in 1983 thus again diversifying its interests.

Like his grandfather, father and brother before him, Mark attended Melbourne Grammar School. Having completed his final secondary school examination in 1978 he went to Roseworthy Agricultural College but three years later left, after deciding that he did not wish to follow Alister into a career as a winemaker. Instead, he went to Brisbane where he worked as an assistant restaurant manager before returning to Nagambie—the township nearest Tahbilk—and managership of the Royal Mail Hotel.

John Purbrick, after a two-year break to gain experience of wine elsewhere, is now re-involved with Tahbilk as resident marketing director in Sydney, responsible for sales and promotion of its wines.

Eric Purbrick's fiftieth vintage occurred in 1981, making it half a century since the 28-year-old former barrister had arrived from England to preside over the harvest of 1931. It also meant that he had become the senior active winemaker in Victoria. Only two others of the State's vignerons—Eric Thomson, of Best's wines at Great Western, and John Brown senior of Brown Bros. at Milawa—

87

have passed the half-century mark in the number of vintages they have seen. All three remain not rivals but good friends. At the luncheon in the 'new' cellars to commemorate the Purbrick landmark, the Chateau Tahbilk Marsanne of 1953—the first Tahbilk wine ever drunk by the Queen—was on the table and voted by the friends and associates who gathered that day with the Purbrick family to be still in remarkably sound condition.

Among those friends present was another well-known father and son wine pair, J. K. Walker ('Johnnie') Walker and his son Peter of Rhine Castle Wines who had only recently been appointed Chateau Tahbilk's Australia-wide agents. This was about the time, too, when Hugh Johnson, regarded by many as the English-speaking world's foremost wine writer, drank the 1964 Chateau Tahbilk Cabernet Sauvignon in London and was inspired to send Eric Purbrick a brief congratulatory cable: 'I am drinking one bloody marvellous wine'.

In a happy speech in reply to the toasts on the occasion of his 'fiftieth vintage' luncheon, Eric Purbrick said that he had seen many changes during the years and was constrained to add 'not all of them for the better' which, with a legal man's typical tact and diplomacy, he did not outline but which many of his listeners took to be a reference to the prevalent-at-the-time takeovers by big businesses of many of his contemporaries' vineyards and wineries. Those who know Tahbilk and the Purbricks know that he has had offers and approaches for the hands at the helm to be transferred but he has always gently but tenaciously guarded what is his own. They similarly know, that the same firmness of purpose will never change after the guiding hands are no longer his own.

In 1983 the senior of the Purbrick's achieved his eightieth birthday, an event which was marked in several happy ways, not the least rewarding of which was the presentation to him of a silver tray by the President, committee and members of the youthful but perceptive Wine Press Club of Victoria 'in appreciation of his contribution to the wine industry.' He treasures the gift and the thought

that prompted it as much as he does anything that has come his way in the years that he has spent building up what was a virtually neglected vineyard when he took over control of it into a universally accepted Australian wine name, one that has been written about by newspapers and magazines ranging from 'The Times', in London, to the local papers of the district around the 125-year-old winery.

It remains today unquestionably the most written-about, painted, sketched, photographed and televised cluster of buildings and cellars in Australia, a favourite not only with writers, artists and cameramen but an enduring friend to those thousands around the world from the Royal Family to the newly-initiated tyro who have known, loved and cherished its wine.

FRANK DOHERTY
Melbourne, 1985.

89